Passing on the Rites of Passage

African Studies Centre
Research Series
6/1995

Passing on the Rites of Passage

Girls' initiation rites in the context of an urban Roman Catholic community on the Zambian Copperbelt

Thera Rasing

Avebury

Cover photograph: Ceremony during initiation rite (photo by Thera Rasing)

ISBN 1 85972 301 2

In grateful memory of Gertrude (†1993)
my interpreter, without whom this book could
not have been written.

Contents

List of Pictures

List of Models

List of Tables

List of Drawings

Acknowledgements

This book about Catholic women's groups and initiation rites on the Zambian Copperbelt is based on literature and on my fieldwork, which was conducted while I was a student in Women and Development Policy. After I came back from fieldwork, I shifted from the study on Women and Development Policy to a study in Anthropology. This book is a revised version of my M.A. thesis which was written to obtain a degree in Anthropology.

In the long process of preparing for and conducting fieldwork, and writing this book many people have helped me in different ways. I would like to thank Prof. van Binsbergen for his supervision and for establishing contacts in Zambia. During the process of writing my thesis, he was very stimulating. I appreciate his constuctive criticism on my thesis and comments on the first draft of this book. I would also like to thank Fr. Jun Gayomali for his supervision and support in Zambia. He followed my work with interest and encouragement.

I am grateful to Sister Ann and Sister Theresa of the Holy Rosary Sisters for the accommodation, their care, their great interest and the information they provided me with. I thank Fr. Jocus Casas for his interest, and many joyful conversations.

Much gratitude is due to Gertrude, who took the difficult task upon herself of interpreting the interviews and discussions for me and providing me with considerable information. I was very sad when the unhappy news reached me that she had died nine months after I left Zambia.

Furthermore I thank all the women's church groups and women without whom this research would not have been possible. I am grateful to all those whom I interviewed and who agreed that I could attend their meetings and an initiation rite.

I would like to thank the Bwalya family, for their accommodation and care, particularly their daughter Christina, who alas passed away very unexpectedly, three weeks after my departure.

I am grateful to Sister Rosalia for the translations of the marriage preparation programmes from Chibemba into English. Only a small part of it could be included in this book. I thank Regina Kanyanja for her translations of the songs from Chibemba into English. I am indebted to John Escott for his checks on the English texts.

I thank the "Vrouwen VU Hulp" (Free University Women's Help), the department of Cultural Anthropology and Sociology of Development of the Vrije Universiteit and the Central Mission Commissariat for their financial contribution.

In conclusion I would like to thank Bert for the lay-out and for all his support, which has been of great importance for me.

Introduction

This book is about Catholic women's groups and initiation rites on the Zambian Copperbelt, incorporating fieldwork conducted from July to October 1992. During this fieldwork I became so much interested in cultural complexities, rituals and human behaviour, that I shifted from a study on Women and Development Policy to a study in Anthropology.

Studying initiation rites poses certain problems due to the sensitive nature of the topic. In a short term, three months, as stipulated by the Vrije Universiteit (Free University) in Amsterdam, I had to find and gain the confidence of women able to discuss the subject with me. Through my supervisor, contact was established with UNZA, the university of Lusaka, Zambia. After initial correspondence, UNZA disapproved of my research proposal, reasoning that the Catholic church was so negative about initiation rites that they were no longer performed; and if the rites still existed, they were performed in secret, not in church. The space of a few months was also judged too short for adequate insight into these matters.

Pressing the investigation proved these assumptions to be false. Initiation rites are still performed, even in towns, and even in the context of a church. Furthermore, I was able to find willing sources during my fieldwork, which allowed me to gather significant materials and grasp the topic within the scheduled period.

Girls' initiation rites are dominant kinship rites, even more than initiation rites for boys. For nearly a century, girls' initiation rites have been banned as pagan and immoral by Roman Catholic missionaries in Zambia. The missionaries proposed no substitute, however, and the traditional rites persisted in secret, circumscribed by time limits. Today, the church has changed its point of view and tries to revitalise and re-evaluate initiation rites.

In this book, I discuss girls' initiation rites, or rites of passage, in an urban Roman Catholic community in Zambia today. Using the word *church*, I refer specifically to the Roman Catholic church. Women's church groups are lay groups centred around a church, and these groups perform initiation rites. How and why they do this, in the context of a church, is the main subject of this book. Thus the central question in this book is:

> *What do rites of passage mean for urban women, and how are women who participate in women's church groups involved in rites of passage?*

Subsidiary questions are:
- By what authority do Christian women perform initiation rites?
- What is the opinion of the clergy about initiation rites, as opposed to popular opinion?
- What is the relevance of initiation rites in towns?

Scant literature exists dealing with initiation rites in an urban environment. An article by Van Binsbergen (1987c) about initiation rites in Lusaka is an exception. Although women in towns have different lives compared to women in villages, initiation rites remain important for urban women. The rites clearly assist the construction of womanhood. Discovering what this means in the perspective of women in a changing society is the main purpose of this book.

Women make use of the church to perform initiation rites. Jules-Rosette (1980) contributes an article about initiation rites in Independent churches, and Verstraelen-Gilhuis (1982) mentions experiments with initiation rites among women in the Reformed church. Initiation rites in the Catholic context however have not been studied before by anthropologists.

In diverse churches there is an ongoing debate about enculturation. Enculturation attempts to combine traditional and Christian values. The tendency is rather toward the Christianisation of traditional customs and values. Marriage and initiation rites are important items in these discussions. Since initiation rites are a part of and a precondition for marriage, the church wants to intervene. This book aims to contribute to the debates about initiation rites raised among missionaries and African priests.

The church constantly seeks new ways to hold its converts. During Vaticanum II the church paid much attention to enculturation and dialogue. After preaching the gospel, missionaries and local priests also direct themselves to topics of development and self-reliance. Regarding enculturation, the clergy selects items to fit in the liturgy. An important item is initiation rites, which the clergy seeks to re-evaluate and modify in accordance to church values. Some priests claim the re-evaluation is necessary because the rites were previously misunderstood, interpreted as a stimulant to amoral sexual behaviour, whereas today the rites are recognised as a procedure that may help maintain moral standards. High rates of teenage pregnancy are attributed to a lack of initiation rites. It is assumed that initiation rites may help prevent unmarried girls from participating in sexual relationships, which can lead to pregnancy or sexually transmitted diseases (STD), particularly AIDS. Nevertheless, the clergy generally regards initiation rites as oppressive for women, teaching them to be subservient. Intervention by the clergy represents an effort to liberalise concepts of sexuality and marriage in a woman's life. Analysing the performance and meaning of the traditional rites may provide insights that help the clergy develop its views further.

Churches in Africa try to change Western, hierarchical structures into self-reliant churches. Ideas about the church's role in enculturation vary, depending on the background of the priest, (e.g. European, African), the seminary he attended, and his age. Some priests do not want enculturation. Others say more indigenous elements ought to be included. This book may help heal this divided atmosphere and encourage enculturation, allowing African traditions and values into the body of Christianity.

Zambian women now find themselves members of a world religion, which has altered their way of living and thinking, creating an existential problematic of alienation and symbolic erosion that sets them searching for specific roots in their own culture. Initiation rites can help to create a community, leading to a sense of order that is helpful particularly in towns, where urbanisation leads to cultural disorientation (Shorter 1991, 26). Communities of women create order and keep up their traditions by performing female initiation rites.

The population in the urbanised Copperbelt consists of several ethnic groups originally from different areas in Zambia, Zaire and Tanzania. The Bemba are the largest ethnic group (Epstein 1958, 5), and Copperbelt Chibemba became the lingua franca.

In the township of Luangwa, where I conducted fieldwork, the population consists mainly of people from the Northern, Eastern and Luapula provinces of Zambia. The majority identify ethnically as Bemba. Others are related to the Bemba and originally speak the same language (Chibemba). The subjects in this book are from the Bemba-speaking people, comprising different groups with many similarities (cf. Richards 1939, 16–17; Epstein 1958, 5–6).

Initiation rites are also rites of passage (cf. Van Gennep 1909). In rites of passage the initiate changes from one state of being into another. The rites may correspond to birth, puberty, marriage or death. Such rites are also called life crisis rites, and may also be employed for the installation of a chief or king. Initiation rites are usually performed when a subject enters a new group. To become a full member, the subject has to undergo certain ritual experiences, which is a familiar feature of rites of passage in general. Often the term initiation is used, when actually rite of passage is meant. In this book I use both.

In chapter one I describe the problems and methods of research, including remarks about my first fieldwork experience and the social circumstances at the time.

The fieldwork setting on the Copperbelt and particularly one of its townships, Luangwa, is described in chapter two, where I also discuss the organisation of the Roman Catholic church and the women's church groups.

Church congregations are comprised of different ethnic groups, and in urban settings these groups mingle. However, since the majority of the population in Luangwa claimed to be Bemba or related to the Bemba, I focus on Bemba culture, which is discussed in chapter three.

In chapter four I outline the theoretical framework and general structure of initiation rites.

The initiation rite I witnessed is described in chapter five. This chapter is much longer than the others since the rite is described in detail, accompanied by explanations offered by the women performing it. This chapter emphasises the personal involvement and experience of the researcher. The rite was performed by members of a women's church

4

group. This is only one example of an initiation rite and is not necessarily representative of all initiation rites occurring in this context.

In chapter six I analyse why initiation rites are still performed in towns, and why they are performed by Catholic women. I also observe the role played by the church, and what priests and sisters think of initiation rites.

1

The Problem and Method of Research

1.1. The problem

Much research has already been done into women's church groups in South Central Africa (e.g. Gaitskell 1990, Lagerwerf 1984 and 1990, Muzorewa 1975). Mostly it has concerned groups of independent churches, but also Protestant churches and to a lesser extent Catholic groups. These groups are cast in a western mould. Initiation rites for girls have also been the subject of much research (e.g. Richards 1956, Turner 1967, La Fontaine 1986). However, as far as I know no research has ever been done into Catholic women's groups performing initiation rites. Consequently this research is largely exploratory, although it has some explanatory elements. In this book the central question is:

> *What do rites of passage mean for urban women and how are women who participate in women's church groups involved in rites of passage?*

Subsidiary questions are:
- By what authority do Christian women perform initiation rites?
- What does the clergy think about initiation rites, as opposed to popular opinion?
- What is the relevance of initiation rites in towns?

Initially I based myself on the assumption that the church was negative about initiation rites and that the church is a highly structured institution that mainly aims at the religious field. Both assumptions were true before Vatican II (1962-1965), but are only partly true today. The church is a hierarchical bulwark but increasingly the power of priests is delegated to the laity and church organisations that claim to be more democratically orientated.

The hypothesis that the church would hold negative views about initiation rites proved to be incorrect. During the Second Vatican Council a start was made at re-evaluating cultural customs (Dondeyne 1967, 149, 159, 160; Flannery 1975, 310, 964-967). Initiation rites are among these. Since that time some priests have tried to combine the initiation rites for girls with ceremonies in church. Thus the initiation rite is allowed (and) christianised. However, combining these rites with church ceremonies has not really worked out because in general women keep the initiation rites hidden, in particular from priests. I will return to this in chapter six.

Nevertheless, from the part of the church, priests and sisters told me that Zambian women who want to join a religious order and have not experienced an initiation rite when they were young, have to be initiated before they can enter. The Zambian sisters I interviewed claimed to have had an initiation rite themselves before entering, which they said was the same as the usual initiation rite for girls. All this, to gain full access to the world of women that is commonly the working area of these nuns.

In my research I based myself on the perspective of autonomy, which is strongly used in women's studies. Gradually I discovered this was not the right starting point for this research. Autonomy is a western concept that can hardly be used in Zambian society. Van Wesemael-Smit states in her article on "Autonomy and Women's Groups" (1988, 269) that autonomy is a relative concept. Autonomy means having control over one's own life and body, by which respect for others and the structures in society remain guaranteed. Autonomy puts the individual in the centre, but is also based on collective supervision in forming a society. In every society various ideal images exist, which do not always put the individual in the centre. Thus autonomy has to be regarded in the context of a certain society in which there may be limits on its attainment.

Some concepts turned out to be hard to translate well into Chibemba. Even with the assistance of an interpreter, questions about women's "rights" did not translate well, because "right/privilege" at the same time means "duty/obligation" in Chibemba (*nsambu*). This is often the case in traditional societies: if one has the right to something that creates obligations too, e.g. if one achieves the right to be leader, one is at the same time obliged to perform that leadership well. If, to clarify my intention, I used stronger words, e.g. law, justice, jurisdiction (*nsambu* and *maka*), these did not convey the correct meaning either, so I decided to leave out questions about this issue, and to concentrate more on initiation rites.

In the past initiation rites were important in the lives of women, and they still are. By experiencing this rite of passage, a woman was legally entitled to bear children. She was seen as an adult and required the privileges and duties that adulthood offered. Priests have opposed against initiation rites, and it is still a subject that is discussed in the church and by the clergy.

1.2. Selection and size of the research population

The focus of this study is on Catholic women's groups in one congregation of the Roman-Catholic church. The church and lay-groups have increasing influence on the lives of women, particularly in the cities. Ever more people live in a town, where customs are more inclined to change, in accordance with the circumstances, than in the villages. In the villages customs also change, albeit at a slower pace, due to the continuous migration between cities and villages.

The area of study was the Copperbelt, because it is a large urbanised area. My research took place in a township, Luangwa, an urban environment near the city of Kitwe. This township was the largest of the Catholic parish of Luangwa. My local supervisor lived here and through him I was easily able to establish contacts with women's groups.

A small research was conducted in the Northern Province, from where most of the inhabitants of the township originated. In the small towns of Kasama, Mpika and Chinsali and in the rural environment of Ilondola, I held some interviews with women of church groups, priests, sisters and development workers involved in women's projects.

There were nine women's groups in Luangwa, viz. Militia, Pioneers, Actio (officially called Catholic Action), Senior Christian Workers, Tertiaries, Nazarethi and three groups of Legio (A,B,C) (officially called Legion of Mary) (see table opposite page 16). All these groups aim at praying, reading the Bible and taking care of the poor and destitute. In addition to this, the Pioneers proclaim total abstinence, and the Nazarethi held discussions about the position of women. I have drawn all groups into my research. Except for the Legion of Mary A, that met once a week, all groups met twice a week. The Actio's meetings diminished while I was there and in the last weeks of my stay there were no meetings at all, mainly due to a lack of members and good leadership, so less attention was devoted to this group. I Sometimes a group had a short meeting, and in such cases I went to the meeting of another group that went on longer. I attended 34 meetings in total.[1]

In addition, I attended a meeting with deputies of all groups twice. One group was the "committee for the poor", the other called itself the "Women's League". Furthermore I attended a meeting of the Parish Council, the body that controls the course of affairs in the parish. I also attended a district meeting of the Legion of Mary once, in order to see how lay groups are organised at the district level.

Luangwa is divided by the Catholic church into eight sections or Christian communities (*fitente*). These sections play an important role in organising the church. I will return to this in chapter two. There are basic similarities in the orientations between the sections and the women's church groups. A difference is that the sections aim at working for all Catholics and have both male and female members, while the women's groups predominantly consist of female members. It is preferred by the clergy that in future the latter will lose their relevance and the sections will be more dominant and active. For that reason I have drawn these sections into my research. Originally I had only intended to examine women's groups as I thought the sections were less relevant to my topic of research. Halfway through, however, I realised that I should use these in my research as well, but for lack of time and practical reasons – all sections have their

---

[1] Viz. Legion of Mary A, B and C four times, Militia four times, Pioneers five times, Senior Christian Workers six times, Actio three times (one very briefly), Tertiaries four times, Nazarethi eight times. This unequal distribution was mainly caused by the fact that the groups sometimes left for a funeral or a retreat. Also, most groups had their meetings at the same time. Only the Nazarethi had a meeting once a week at a time when there were no other meetings.

meetings at the same time – I had to restrict myself to three sections. Two of these sections I chose on the advice of my local supervisor because they function well. The third I selected on the basis of being a less well functioning and thus more typical section. Observation during the meetings was the main technique. I attended seven meetings, viz. Saint Anthony three times, Saint Andrew twice and Saint Francis twice.

I interviewed 39 women, 34 of whom were in Luangwa and five in the Northern Province. Seven women from Luangwa were interviewed twice, two women three times and one five times. I started interviewing the chairladies and further I took an a-select group. Some women I selected purposely, because they held a specific position in the parish.

I also intended to interview girls who had just finished their initiation or were about to have it soon. It turned out to be very difficult to talk about initiation rites with these girls, because during the initiation they are taught not to speak about it with anyone. Even the girl whose initiation I attended did not want to talk about it. For that reason I attended some meetings of the adolescents' group, the Youfra. This group consists of both boys and girls between 17 and 25 years of age. All the girls had had their initiation rite, except one girl who was a Ngoni, for whom an initiation rite is not such a big celebration as for the Bemba. The initiation rites had taken place in the years between 1980 and 1986.

In addition, I interviewed three girls. One of them was about to get married in the traditional way. I interviewed her twice. The second was an unmarried mother and the last one had been pregnant while not being married and had given still-birth two weeks before the interview.

I interviewed four European priests, three Zambian priests and a Kenyan priest. I further interviewed four European sisters, three Zambian sisters and a Ghanaian sister. The priests and sisters I had partly selected myself, partly I was directed to them by my local supervisor and some of the priests and sisters.
I also conducted some interviews with people from organisations that are concerned with the position of women or who are working with a Catholic organisation.[2] With some of these organisations I had established contact in the preparatory phase. To some other organisations I was directed by organisations and priests I already had interviewed.

---

[2]   These were:

NGOCC (Non Governmental Organisations Co-ordinating Committee Lusaka)		once
ZARD (Zambian Association for Research and Development) Lusaka		once
Catholic Secretariat Lusaka		once
Family Life Movement Lusaka		twice
Family Life Movement Kitwe		three times
Mindolo Ecumenical Foundation,	head of women's courses	twice
	head of social work	once
ALM (Association of Lay Members)		once
CHEP (Copperbelt Health Education Program)		twice
Marriage Encounter,	leading married couple	once
	participant	once

1.3. Collecting data

Data were gathered by participant observation and more or less formal interviewing. The interviews with the women were both structured interviews supported by questionnaires and unstructured interviews (see appendix A). During the interviews I was assisted by an interpreter except with two women who spoke English well. The interviews with priests, sisters and employees of organisations were structured interviews supported by a questionnaire. During these interviews I was able to dispense with the interpreter.

Participating in the church groups was hardly possible, because these meetings mainly consisted of praying and speeches by the chairpersons. Moreover, in most groups nobody could speak English, so I could not be drawn into the conversation and I mainly observed. At these group meetings, I mainly observed, with my interpreter translating. Usually I asked questions to the chairladies at the end of the meeting. The meetings of the women's church groups sometimes took a long time, about three to four hours. Frequently the same subjects were discussed and I soon learned that verbosity and repeating oneself and others is very common. Moralising addresses were given and verbal punishments inflicted.

The discussions with the women's groups were done in connection with a questionnaire I handed out to all groups. This was arranged in advance. These questionnaires had been translated into Chibemba by my interpreter. There were only two groups that started working on it seriously. After a conversation with my local supervisor it turned out that they could only fill up the questionnaires after approval by the Parish Council. I did not know this in advance. I had actually taken the hierarchical route from the missionary through the chairpersons to the group members, but missed the step of the Parish Council. In later meetings, the questions were discussed and the questionnaires were filled up. Two groups did not answer the questions: the Tertiaries did not want to co-operate because their chairperson was absent for a while, and the Action had no more meetings. The Legion of Mary A, B and C answered one questionnaire together. It was difficult to make good plans as to with which group I could attend the discussion because most groups had their meeting at the same time and some meetings were cancelled for funerals and retreats or for lack of attending members. I attended three out of five group discussions. These discussions are recorded on cassette tape. I also took notes. Afterwards I had conversations with the chairladies about the answers they had given in order to go into the subject more deeply.

The discussions with the Youfra were in connection with questionnaires too. I had made separate questionnaires for boys and girls, and the group was split while answering the questions. I had four discussions with the girls and one with the whole group. The matters discussed were sexuality, future marriage and initiation rites. This was difficult, particularly for the girls, which shows that it is a taboo to talk about these things in public with representatives of the other sex. However, it seemed that boys were more willing to talk about this and to "break" this taboo. The discussions were partly in Chibemba, partly in English.

The announcements after the services, which were translated by my interpreter, supplied me with information about the workings of the parish. Furthermore I twice attended a part of the meeting of the pastoral team.

The information about initiation rites, described in chapter 5, is based on my observations during the initiation rite that I attended, and on the interviews with the *banacimbusa* (midwife or mentrix) who performed this rite. I recorded the initiation rite on tape and also took notes.

Moreover, I had many informal conversations with the priests and sisters of the pastoral team, the chairman of the Parish Council, the family where I was lodged, my interpreter and several other women.

1.4. Working with an interpreter

As I could not speak the local language, the lingua franca of the Copperbelt, I had to work with an interpreter. Working with an interpreter did not pass off without difficulties due to the circumstances. However, through contact with her, and all the information she provided me with, I learned a lot about the culture and cultural behaviour. I was taught of the importance of being married, of having children, of being employed, and what is means to be a working class woman in this society.

Because the research was about church groups and initiation rites, and sexuality would be a regular subject of conversation, the interpreter had to be a woman who had passed the initiation rite herself, had to be married and have children and had to have a Catholic background. In the township only a few people met with these conditions and could also speak English well.

My interpreter was not married in the traditional way, so according to her, this was a disadvantage and it held back people from talking openly about initiation and sexuality. I am not sure whether that really was the case. Rather I think holding back was caused by the ideas about me that prevailed among the people. Another drawback was that she had to look after her children so she was not always available.

She was also ill for a while, so for over two weeks she could only work 50 percent of the time. During that period I looked for another interpreter. Two young women were willing to help me, but neither of them was married nor had children, so to me they did not seem fit to the job. Besides, I felt a bond of loyalty towards my interpreter, so we decided to finish the research together.

After three months of pleasant and good co-operation, some strain arose. I found out she sometimes did not interpret everything and dropped information she considered to be useless. Usually, a few days before an interview I made an appointment with the people I wanted to interview. In the beginning this worked out very well but later it did not. This disappointed me. The custom is to visit one another spontaneously. That was what I liked best, but according to my interpreter that was not possible. I think she wanted to make clear that she did not want to do it this way herself. Neither did she want to visit a certain woman who, in my opinion, could provide me with much information and who was eager to do so. It turned out that she accused this woman of witchcraft and was afraid of her.

The long hours of interpreting, caring for her children, and, on top of that, her physical weakness, became too much of a load. Suddenly we had a crisis and I realised I had underestimated the task and the work she had done for me. In the beginning I wanted to agree upon a financial reward with her, but she herself, my local supervisor, and the chairladies who were involved said that "a little something" would do, because "we are Christians, so we help each other without having to be paid." Only later did I understand this was more an expression than that it was really meant. So it came to an open conflict. Later I realised, that, although occasionally conflicts come out into the open, it is not in accordance with the culture and it puts the people concerned in a bad light. We talked it over and both admitted that we had made mistakes. I think the conflict has had little effect on my research, especially because we were seen together soon afterwards.

In general my interpreter was nice to get on with. She was a confidential agent to me. However, my dependence on her made things difficult for me. I experienced the unfamiliarity with the language as a severe handicap. But working with an interpreter provided me with a lot of information about cultural behaviour.

1.5. My position as a field worker

In addition to the usual problems faced in fieldwork (cf. Ten Have 1977), I encountered problems deriving from my inexperience in doing fieldwork. As I did not have an anthropological background, and I had hardly had any fieldwork training, I did not exactly know what participant observation meant and what it contained. This explains for a good deal the problems I had during interviewing and with my interpreter. Besides, there was a problem of language. Only two women, apart from my interpreter, spoke English, and I did not speak nor understand the lingua franca, Chibemba. As my background was on women's studies, my point of departure was on women's groups. Only later I found out that I had to see them in a wider context and to take into account their history.

For many people the aim of my stay was obscure. Just after my arrival in Luangwa, I was introduced to the parish by the missionary who also was my local supervisor. This happened the first time during the Sunday-mass, as with every visitor, and afterwards twice in a group where all deputies of women's church groups were present. Father Gayomali explained the purpose of my stay. In spite of his explanation and my own explanation afterwards in all groups separately, and even, initially, during the interviews, the purpose of my presence was unclear to most people.

In the opinion of Father Gayomali, research into Catholic women and initiation rites could benefit these women and their position in the church, and could facilitate the process of enculturation. However, for the people it remained unclear whether the missionary, who is seen as the highest local authority, fully agreed with my research. How indistinct this was for Luangwa's inhabitants only became clear after three months, when the chairman and the secretary of the Parish Council wanted an interview with the missionary and me. It was mainly because they had heard of my interest in initiation rites and the fact that a few women's groups had offered to set up a fake initiation ceremony merely for the benefit of my research. I did not want this because it was going to be too artificial, but the rumour that a ceremony was to be organised for me was going about. They were suspicious about my intentions with the information. Several times already I had spoken with the chairman of the Parish Council about my research, but apparently it had not been enough. Only during this interview did it become clear to them that the missionary fully agreed with my study, and they approved of my research. Later on I was allowed to attend an initiation rite, which was not made up for me, but was for the occasion of a particular girl who had become mature.

At first, many women told me about the problems with their husbands, particularly about the fact that they did not give them enough money, their frequently being drunk, and the many unwanted pregnancies while they already had many children. A few times, as I thought it would be possible, I asked them if they could not do anything against it, and if so, what they could do. Right now I think that question was posed from a western point of view.

The first two months I lived at the sisters' place and thus many people associated me with the church. In my opinion, this largely explains the answers of most people, in which they repeatedly claimed to be a member of a group, to work for God, referring to the Bible. I expressed the wish to stay with a family. This appeared to be very difficult, mainly owing to the fact that the people were cramped for space but in the end it worked out. My privacy was limited, but I got a better insight into the workings of a household and family life.

A few times women invited me spontaneously. Mostly this lead to an interview. One time it went wrong and again it appeared that the aim of my stay in Luangwa was not clear to everyone. Two elderly women invited me in. I mostly visited those who asked me to come, or I asked someone who I thought was willing to narrate. The two women talked a lot about the church lay group, of which they were members. As the interview flagged, I asked some things about initiation rites. They answered my questions reluctantly. It was considered very impolite to ask elderly persons questions.

I used to work on my notes far into the night. This made me very tired and I sometimes found it hard to cope. Over and over again, I tried to interview and attend group meetings, so I hardly got round to any rest. To me rest was identical with stagnation. In retrospect I think taking a break would have been better to let everything settle down, to recover my breath and to proceed with new courage. Also the time limit played me tricks. I felt continuous strain and did not allow myself the time for a day of doing "nothing". These elements of doing fieldwork are also described by Van Binsbergen (1987c).

The women did not see me as a woman, but as a young girl who needed protection. Participating was made difficult. At first it was experienced as strange that I wanted to do particular things. I was not to accompany the women to the well or to the bush; that would be too far a walk for me and carrying water was too heavy. Besides, a guest was not supposed to do such things. Gradually participating became more appreciated and I was allowed to cook and fetch water with them. I learned that at festivities one does not only act as a spectator, but also as a participant in e.g. dancing, singing or worshipping aloud.

The African perception of the body is different from that of the European perception. In their eyes I seemed very young and people called my looks childlike. Besides it was assumed I was not married nor had any children. For this reason I was not taken seriously, because young, unmarried and childless women have low status. For these women it was enough reason not to tell me too much about women's affairs and sexuality. A change in their attitude towards me occurred when I told them I was married. I was not married in the formal (western) way, but in Zambia different kinds of marriages are common today, in particular in urban area's. Having a steady relationship with a man can also imply being married. Afterwards the women discussed various subjects "openly" with me. I was even given the opportunity to attend an initiation rite, despite the secrecy of the initiation rites for the non-initiated.

1.6. Drought and social circumstances

During my stay in Zambia, parts of the country, including my study area of the Copperbelt, as well as other parts of Southern Africa, were struck by drought. Because of the increasing lack of water, women had to walk further and further and wait longer and longer at the well or the only spring that still contained a little water. The strongly polluted river was far away for many. As I arrived at the river, people used to ask me whether I was investigating the water supply.

I think that the lack of water was one of the reasons why the willingness to talk with me was decreasing. The women did not want me to accompany them to the well because they thought it was too far for me to walk. Perhaps they had other reasons as well. They might not be back in time, had less time for the rest of their domestic tasks, or were too tired. Another reason was the custom of offering food to a visitor, food they could hardly afford for themselves. Food parcels were distributed, but these were only for the poorest. Between the announcement and the actual distribution several weeks elapsed. During these weeks this was the main subject of conversation and a few meetings of the women's groups were cancelled.

At the same time, many meetings and interviews were cancelled on account of the many funerals. When a family member or an inhabitant of the group member's neighbourhood, or a group member from another township of the parish passes away, it is usual that the whole group attend the funeral. Usually the group stays one morning or one afternoon. The funeral itself usually takes two days. I do not have statistical data at my disposal about the number of deceased, so I do not know whether there were more funerals than during other periods. According to the missionaries and the sisters more meetings than usual were cancelled because of funerals.

The changing of the season into the beginning of the dry and hot season played a role as well. All this, together with ongoing inflation and continuous rises in prices, made the people anxious. They had many things to worry about. Nevertheless, they informed me about initiation rites and other customs, so I was able to conduct my fieldwork.

Despite all these problems concerning the social circumstances, I went on with interviewing and attending meetings of the church groups, instead of participating more and trying to see what these people were concerned about and what they did during their daily life. That would have given me a better opportunity to understand these people and their culture, but at least I had made a start at learning how to do fieldwork, and this has formed a basis for further research.

Now that the method of research and the social circumstances during my fieldwork are explained, in the next chapter the urban environment of the research will be described. I will discuss the Copperbelt and the township of Luangwa. I will also describe the organisation of Luangwa Catholic church, its women's groups and Christian communities.

2

The Copperbelt and its Social and Religious Organisation

In this chapter I will describe the Copperbelt and one of its townships, Luangwa, where the fieldwork was conducted. I will deal with social networks on the Copperbelt, in particular the church and the church lay groups.

2.1. The Copperbelt

In 1889 Zambia (then Northern Rhodesia) became part of the British South African Company and in 1924 it became a British Protectorate. Under the pressure of head and poll taxes, all able-bodied men had to earn money in the mines or towns as there were few opportunities to sell local products for cash. Both taxations and food shortages forced people to look for work.

When the copper mining companies in Northern Rhodesia began the construction of the mines in 1926, they faced a shortage of black labour. The Copperbelt mines had to compete with other mines in Southern Africa, which permitted miners to bring their wives and children to the mines. The Copperbelt companies were reluctant to hire married labourers because of the costs of housing and feeding women and children (Parpart 1983, 3). As the mining companies began to recognise the profitability of a more skilled and stable black labour force, they became increasingly committed to hiring married labourers (Parpart 1983, 3).

In the beginning the workers stayed for only a few years, but later on they settled permanently. Many of these men were young and unmarried and not so much needed at the village. According to Walker (1990, 173) it was men who went to work, because women were the main domestic workers and workers in the fields. Besides, for the colonisers with their western concept of labour, it should be men who were working for money.

Through various measures colonial administration made it difficult for a man to take his family with him (Roberts 1976, 74, 183, 188). As a result of the declining labour in the rural areas and the increasingly heavy workload for women in the rural areas, (single) women went to the Copperbelt, trying to find a living. They were trying to find a man or engage in prostitution. Women also tried to earn some money by brewing and selling beer.

Chiefs were losing their authority. They co-operated with the government to bring single women back to the rural areas. In the 1930's a woman needed to be married in order to stay with her husband on the Copperbelt and if they did not have a valid certificate, women were removed from the Copperbelt. Marriages were registered. However, many women found someone who was willing to "marry" them. Also, if a woman stayed for one week in a man's house and cooked for him, they were regarded as married (Parpart 1983, 6). In 1944 the mining companies issued passes for unmarried women to visit the compounds. However, the mine police made regular sweeps through the compounds, looking for unauthorised women. Evictions of all unauthorised persons increased in the 1950's, in an effort to isolate the mines from the tumult of African nationalist politics (cf. Epstein 1958, Parpart 1983, 7).

After some strikes, the mining companies and the Northern Rhodesian Government recognised the need for greater control over the labour force. In 1931 the system of tribal elders was installed, which meant that the various ethnic groups had to elect representatives (Epstein 1958, 28). After another strike these elders lost their influence, because they lacked the legal power with which to enforce their authority (Epstein 1958, 32).

The mining companies only wanted women in the compounds as long as it served their purposes. Women assisted their husbands with strikes. The mines became ever more committed to stabilisation and thus to services assisting adjustments to life in the mine compounds. In the 1950's and 1960's married couples were allowed to settle down near the mines. As a result, the towns grew.

The migration of men without their families was a feature all over Southern Africa. Through capitalist expansion the village communities became dependent on the market and incorporated into the money-economy. The dominance of the capitalist mode invariably led to the weakening of old unities of production (Van Binsbergen and Geschiere 1985, 117). However, the capitalist expansion did not bring about the immediate demolition of the old modes of production, but used old modes of production for the further expansion of capitalism (Van Binsbergen and Geschiere 1985, 5). Expanding cash needs and declining rural production made people go in search of work. Because of the overwhelming supply of labour, employment became scarce. As is usual when employment is scarce, the jobs which were still available were given to men. Women were unemployed or tried to work in the informal sector.

The Copperbelt became the most urbanised province in Zambia and a region with a mixed composition, with contrasts between agricultural and pastoral, matrilineal and patrilineal peoples, and groups of different ethnic origin, whether from Zambia or Zaire. The Bemba are one of the largest ethnic groups in the Copperbelt. The Bemba language became the lingua franca of this region.

In 1975, copper mining was reduced because of decreasing demand in the world market and increasing costs of production and transportation. The resulting unemployment is a serious matter of concern, both at a national and a local level.

2.2. The situation of women and men in town

Traditionally a woman provided food for her family through gardening. She was helped by her husband. Economic interdependency consisted of a division of labour based on a domestic mode of production, with bonds marked by reciprocity. Relationships were based on equality between husband and wife, wherein both roles functionally complement each other (Touwen 1984, 14).

When women came to live in town they had to cope with many problems. They had to live without the support of their relatives and also were forced to earn money to keep up their families. The daily life in town emphasised the nuclear family. Besides, the housekeeping, which was done by women, took less time than in the village, where people had to grow crops, fetch water, pound meal etcetera. The men expected their wives to be at home, their houses to be clean, and their meals to be cooked when they came home from work (Epstein 1981, 70).

In both rural and urban areas there was and still is a breakdown of the old family organisation and marriage institutions and an emergence of new marital usages and new social groups (Richards 1940, 7). Town people mixed with other tribes, which also meant that mixed marriages became more common. However, kinship links are still important as emotional bonds between people but seem to be loosing their controlling and economic-supportive function (Touwen 1984, 38).

In town the position of the husband was enhanced. He was now the breadwinner and had the responsibility for providing a house for his wife and children. His wife did the customary duties of caring for the children, cooking and looking after the household (Epstein 1981, 68). Performing these tasks was an expression of the customary fashion, but also an acknowledgement of the husbands new status as breadwinner and master of the household (Epstein 1981, 70). The cooking of food appeared as the woman's contribution to a set of reciprocal and balanced obligations between husband and wife, but it also has to be seen as an expression of the weakened position of the woman vis-à-vis her husband. Traditionally a married couple acquired recognition of their fully independent status only gradually. The young husband spent the first years of his marriage in uxorilocal setting and was depending on his in-laws, while in town the marriage was neolocal and the husband became master of the house immediately.

2.3. Catholic missionaries in Zambia

In 1878 missionaries came to east Africa and made contact with the Bemba in 1891 (Garvey 1977, 412). The presence of the mission was to give expression to tensions in the indigenous relationship between the chiefship and the populace (Comaroff 1905, 150). The missionaries flowed into the cracks of the existing structure: the earliest converts - poor men and women in general - were those who were marginal in terms of indigenous social categories and authoritative relations (Comaroff 1985, 150; Gaitskell 1990, 253). For them, Christianity promised a novel source of influence and control; the mission was a tangible embodiment of force. It also offered a positive social identity: within it, structural marginality was redefined as membership in the society of the saved (Comaroff 1985, 150). Carmody (1988, 20) says that many Zambians became Catholics not because of the supernatural power but for social and economic reasons. Women have benefited from some of the changes the missionaries have brought, while other changes were negative.

The Christian missions were expanded in co-operation with the colonial government. The latter looked upon this familiar and European controlled Christianity as an important factor for order and well-contained progress. They utilised the secular skills, e.g. literacy, which the African converts had acquired in their associations with the missions (Van Binsbergen 1981, 151).

The priests had a negative attitude towards the native culture. It was seen as heathenish. The people were to be civilised, which meant that they should have a western way of life. Missionaries, like all people, are a product of their time. Many aspects of the indigenous culture were abolished. As part of the evangelisation process, people were obliged to give up a wide range of traditional cultural practices, including initiation rites for girls, divination and the honouring of the family and tribal ancestors (Garvey 1977, 417; Oger 1991, 199). Initiation rites were seen as useless and obscene. Many of the things which were forbidden by the missionaries nevertheless went on secretly. My informants claimed that even in the villages the initiation rites continued to be practised, although it was forbidden by the missionaries. Only people who lived near a mission station were unable to perform initiation rites. Garvey (1977, 417) and Oger (1991, 199) mention that the missionaries exerted punishments for having performed an initiation rite, for instance by withholding Holy Communion.

There are many different churches in Zambia, mission churches as well as independent churches. About one quarter of the Zambian population is Catholic (Verstraelen-Gilhuis 1982, 32).

2.4. Luangwa township and Luangwa Catholic Church

Luangwa is situated in the Copperbelt, 10 km from Kitwe town centre. It had a population of approximately 20,000 people in 1990. The annual population growth rate in the area is 4.7% as compared to the national growth rate of 3.2% (Gayomali 1990, 2). Luangwa is regarded as the fastest growing "site and service" township in Kitwe, i.e. an area where officially demarcated plots are being allocated with roads and water, and electricity are provided.

Originally, the people of Luangwa came from squatter areas surrounding Kitwe City and were reallocated to the place during the Squatters Upgrading Programme of the government in the 1970's. The majority of the people came from Northern Province, Eastern Province and Luapula Province. They are mainly retired or unemployed, contract workers in the industrial area of the city of Kitwe, and some are self-employed or indulge in petty trading. Those who are self-employed are either charcoal burners or small handicraft workers. Some people still own small fields which they cultivate near the township. Many people are under-employed and many young people are school drop-outs (Gayomali 1990, 2).

Luangwa Catholic Parish was founded in 1968 by Franciscan missionaries. The parish has been growing since and now consists of eight townships, of which Luangwa is the largest. In 1989 the parish was taken over by the Fathers of the Congregation of the Immaculate Heart of Mary (CICM). The parish is now conducted by the pastoral team which consists of two priests and three sisters. About 25% of the inhabitants of Luangwa is a Catholic (interview with the parish priest).

The pastoral team tries to make the local people aware of the socio-economic and political situation and tries to develop programs so that people can enhance their situation (interview with the parish priest). The Parish Council (*insaka ya parish*) is the umbrella organisation of the parish. It co-ordinates plans, programmes and activities in the parish..

The parish structure in Luangwa has two levels, the parish and the community level. Each community (*citente*, plural *fitente*) is divided into committees, for liturgy, Catechism, finance and youth. Every community has a representative on the Parish Council.

The parish level is composed of the committees (the same as at the *citente* level), and one is added, namely the Mandated organisations (*Mabumba*). These are the church lay (or women's) groups. They are the Legio (A,B,C, officially called Legion of Mary), Militia, Actio (officially called Catholic Action), Tertiaries, Pioneer, Senior Christian Workers, Nazarethi, Children of Mary, Youfra (Young Franciscans) and Stella (church dancing group for children aged 12 to 18). Each group has a representative. They form the committee of the mandated organisations and have a representative on the Parish Council (except the Youfra, Children of Mary and Stella).

During my research, all these groups had to elect representatives, who formed the committee of the poor (*kabungwe kabalanda*). This committee had to look for and look after the poor and the destitute and to decide who should get help, e.g. food supply.

2.5. The Christian Community

Much has been written about the new organisations and networks in urban settings. Most of it is about unions or other political organisations and churches. (See for example Epstein 1964, Harries-Jones 1975, Mitchell 1969, Morrow 1989, O'Shea 1986, Sofer 1964, Verstraelen 1975 and 1976). The United National Independence Party (UNIP) which was founded by Kenneth Kaunda and was the only party when Zambia obtained independence in 1964, tried to organise people. Touwen (1984, 43) claims that although it was the UNIP's policy to create women's leagues in every section, it is difficult to get women interested in membership. Only some highly educated women in the urban environment seem to be interested. Apart from the churches it seems to be difficult to organise women (Touwen 1984, 43).

Of importance in this study is the role of the Catholic church as the main organisation in building a social network in town. This is done by the introduction of Christian communities. They are everywhere in East Africa and founded by the Bishops' Conference (AMECEA) in 1973. In Luangwa there are eight Christian communities (*fitente*), bounded by geographic borders. They were founded in 1991 and had many difficulties initially. Two of them are functioning quite well, the others not so well. This is probably because they have only just started, but I think it is also because they are ordered from above. These communities aim to get more lay participation in the church life.

Each community has a chairperson, *kafwa*, which means helper, to denote that he is not a "boss", but often people, including the "helper", regard him or her as the boss. These communities are more or less similar to the villages with chiefs or headmen. The same division was made by UNIP (Harries-Jones 1975, 109).

Christian communities began as a reaction to the concept of the Catholic church as an impersonal organisation controlled by the hierarchy. They are partly born out of a crisis in Christian ministry, mainly because of the lack of ordained ministers. Healey (1981, 101), a priest with a pastoral view, states that the Christian communities are the church, at the level of the people's life. The purpose of the policy of Christian communities is to ensure that people can practice their Christian faith in places where they work and live, to bring about a greater lay participation and to provoke a more authentic enculturation.

Shorter (1991, 103) states that where the communities started from below, they were successful. Most of the priests I interviewed thought that the concept of Christian community was good, but many of them said that it was difficult to put it in practice. Most priests said that the Christian communities are working well in the towns, but not in the villages. The reason for this is that in the villages the relations between the people are rather intimate, so they do not need the Christian community. In the cities, where people have few or no relatives and life is unknown, people need each other more and often depend on the church for material and emotional support.

The Christian community is an extension of the Catholic church and a way to get involved in the believers' daily life. The vision of the Christian community is that every Christian should be responsible and take care of others and live according to the gospel. The community can decide what is good or not, or what should be done. When one does not stick to the rules which are made by the church and the community, one is an outsider. The community provides control and balance. A member has to pay a certain amount of money and gets free sacraments. When someone moves to another town, a representative of the Christian community sends a letter to introduce this person. When people have marital problems and they were married in church, they will ask help from the priest, the women's lay group or a member of the Christian community. My informants claimed that all people who are mature have a say in the upbringing of children, because they are Christians. Here we see the that the church is trying to create a sense of a community, like a village where all mature people could intervene in the way children are brought up. This influence, which is quite authoritative, might be negative, but can also make life more convenient.

Women and men are supposed to have equal positions in the Christian community, but usually the men are chairpersons and women are just members, or vice-chairpersons. The men organise and moderate, while women do the work in practice. In Luangwa two of the chairpersons of the sections are female, the others are male. About half of the vice persons are men and half are women.

There are similarities in the orientations between the Christian communities and the women's groups. These similarities are often the cause of tensions between the Christian communities and the women's groups. The women's groups are discouraged and the communities are promoted for practical, biblical and theological reasons. These reasons are that the church wants more activities and involvement of people in the area where they live. Women's groups usually gather in church ground and comprising members of different areas of the parish. According to the priests Christian communities are in consonance to the first Christian communities practises. They want people reflecting on their faith experience together while considering their specific geographical situation. In this geographical area there are also non-Catholics.

2.6. The women's church groups

Women's church groups still play an important part in the lives of religious people. Here they study the Bible and pray. They also plan spiritual and social acts, e.g. visiting people who are ill, and activities like the preparation of church festivals. The purpose of these groups is to combine evangelisation with the meaning and implication of the Christian life, especially concerning the family relations of Christians (Lagerwerf 1990, 52).

There are nine women's church groups in Luangwa. They all include men and women, except the Nazarethi, so actually they should be called lay groups, but because there are very few men and to avoid confusing them with other lay groups, I prefer to call them women's groups. All the groups exist where Catholicism has taken root, so they are not only in Zambia, except for the Nazarethi. All the groups have a constitution and rules, which are made and codified by the district council of every group. If one does not stick to them, one will be punished. It seems that people want to have order, both in the groups and in the community. Hardly anyone in the groups knew the constitution, except for the members of the Legion of Mary.

A women's church group offers crisis support, e.g. in cases of illness, death or funerals, which in rural situations is provided by kin or neighbours. A group provides moral and material support and assists individuals with the adaptation to the urban life. It provides its members with a personal network in a city where most relationships for a migrant are new and impersonal. These personal networks are very important for helping people to get in contact with the urban social environment. Whurch women's groups manifest themselves in three different but related ways. They are local formal organisations, they provide material and spiritual assistance, and they are a structure of social control (cf. Lagerwerf 1984; Van Binsbergen 1987a, 15).

Women's church groups control people and keep them up to the moral code imposed by the church, such as monogamy, responsible family life, moderate drinking habits, avoidance of criminal behaviour (Lagerwerf 1990, 52, Van Binsbergen 1987a, 17, West 1975). In controlling these standards the church is not only protecting its membership quota but is also exerting a more general form of social control, which is all the more important in the urban environment.

Although imitating essential elements of traditional kinship and marital structures, the church offers not a continuation but an alternative (Van Binsbergen 1987a, 18). The church takes on this fictive kinship role not only because of lack of kinsmen in town. In Luangwa many recent urban migrants can in fact make use of kin-based reception structures when looking for housing and employment. For two or three generations they live in Luangwa now. They are used to urban forms and seem to insist on social control and domestic conflict regulation. The women's group takes over the forms and patterns of social relations as in the rural areas in order to articulate itself as an alternative fictive kin structure. A factor in the reliance on the alternatives offered by the church is that the urbanites involved are past the stage where they would seek and accept rural intervention (Van Binsbergen 1987a, 22).

A women's church group gives the women status and authority. Many people are members of a group, and relatives, for instance daughters or sisters are often members of different church groups. Being a chairlady gives them particular power and status. The chairlady is chosen by the members. The main condition for being a chairlady is to be married in church. A church wedding gives prestige and in this way she makes an example to the members.

All the women's church groups have some traditional midwives among them, who are called *banacimbusa*. A *banacimbusa* has much knowledge about traditional customs and she is entitled to perform initiation rites for girls. She also leads the wedding ceremony and assists the young woman whom she has initiated when the latter gives birth to her first child. A *banacimbusa* is never of the same kingroup as the girl she initiates and she is treated with great respect.

All the members of the groups said that their main purpose is to help the poor and destitute and to pray. However, the main comment from the priests on these groups is that they do not actually help. They are discussing problems between husband and wife or neighbours, without talking about the things underneath, which are the real causes of the problems. E.g. the Pioneers are against the drinking of alcohol, but they do not discuss the real problems of why people drink. Another comment is that they do not develop themselves, meaning that they should develop according to European norms. However, development along these lines is not their purpose.

All women said that in their lay group they are improving their position. By improving they mean making sure that their husbands stay with them. As they say "one is really poor, if one does not have a husband". This is not only for financial reasons or for procreation, but because the social status of a woman depends on her marital status. Thus a woman without a husband has a low social status. To make sure that the husband stays with her, the wife has to do everything to please him. Therefore she has to learn how to behave, how to cook properly and how to act in a sexual relationship. This she learns during the initiation and the wedding ceremony and is also discussed in most of the church lay groups, because "they have to learn" and "people forget what they have learned". It is remarkable that in the perception of these women, traditional values, as they exist in the villages, and the strategies women use to survive in town, are mingled.

These women's groups have many similarities. Because of the change in my research from women's groups to rites of passage, I will not describe these groups in length. An overview of the church lay groups in Luangwa is given in the table below.

One women's church group, the Nazarethi, which follows the footsteps of Saint Elizabeth, was founded to revitalise traditional customs, in particular initiation rites for girls. In this thesis I will focus on initiation rites which are performed by this group. Since initiation rites focus on basic values of the people concerned, I will first explain which these values are. The women who performed the rite which I have attended claimed it to be a Bemba rite. Although there are many similarities in the customs of different people in South-Central Africa, I will concentrate on Bemba values and describe Bemba customs in the next chapter.

Table of women's church groups in Luangwa

	Militia (M.I. Mary Immaculate)	Legio A (Legion of Mary)	Legio B	Legio C	SCW Senior Christian Workers	Pioneers	Actio (Catholic Action)	Nazarethi	Tertiaries (Third order of the Franciscans)
Members f / m	47 33 / 14	40 32 / 8	40 females only	32 27 / 5	73 60 / 13	80 55 / 25	45 37 / 8	67 females only	30-40 the exact number was not registered
Average members at meeting	20	25	23	20	23	15 (women only) 25 (mixed)	8	40	6
Year of foundation	1917 Zambia 1980 Luangwa	1922 Dublin 1974 Luangwa				1898 Dublin 1958 Zambia 1981 Luangwa	1930 Europe 1935 Zambia 1970 Luangwa	1953 Mufulira (Copperbelt) 1968 Luangwa	
Purpose	movement of Church and a Marian apostolate for all Catholics; help the poor and destitute.	attend every meeting; stick to the gospel; pray the Rosary every day, because this is the chain of the Legion of Mary; be active; do all the work in the name of Christ and Mary; all things discussed in the group have to be kept secret from outsiders.			workers for God; work; discuss problems; obey; offenders will be punished.	abstain from alcohol; to abolish drinking of alcohol because it leads to many problems; help the poor and destitute.	help the poor and the destitute; preach the gospel.	teach traditional values; revalue initiation rites, in Christian way; teach to be banacimbusa; help poor and destitute and couples with marital problems.	help the poor and destitute.
Chair-person	female	female	female	female	female (meetings with only women) male (mixed meetings)	female	male	female	male
Elections	every 2 years	every 2 years			every 3 years	every 2 years	every 2 years	every 2 years	every 3 years
Uniform	badge with MI on it	none			green head-dress	red head-dress and badge	none	white head-dress	they used to have a brown uniform with a cord, now they have no features
Attributes	N/A	small altar with a cloth that says Legion of Mary a statue of Mary, two vases with flowers			once a week they used a stool as an altar with a green cloth and a drawing of Christ	N/A	N/A	N/A	N/A
Meetings per week	2: 1 only women, 1 mixed	2: 1 only women, 1 mixed	1: only women	2: 1 only women, 1 mixed	2: 1 only women, 1 mixed	2: 1 only women, 1 mixed on Sunday they sing the Pioneers Song in front of the church altar	2: 1 only women, 1 mixed	2: 1 to discuss family life, 1 to discuss the poor	2: 1 only women, 1 mixed
Remarks		The constitution says that no more than 40 members are allowed in any one group. Therefore there are 3 groups.					Towards the end of my stay hardly anyone came to the meetings so there were no meetings anymore. Reason: funerals, and the chairperson was a man, so on the meeting for the women he was not present and on mixed meetings people did not come.	Every member has to be married in church.	Members are not allowed to remarry once they are widow or widower The meetings were unstructured, both when the chairman was present and when there were only women. It was announced in church that people could join them but with no result. By the time I left Luangwa there were hardly any meetings.

3

Bemba Culture

In this chapter I will describe traditional Bemba customs and world-view in which marriage is a central item. These customs and world-view are more or less common all over South Central Africa. Yet I will call them "Bemba" customs because there are some differences in comparison with neighbouring groups. Most of these values are expressed in the initiation rite, which I will describe in the next two chapters. In order to understand the initiation rite the traditional culture has to be described first.

Anthropological studies which are done in the past (1930's and 1940's) are valuable in describing traditional customs. They set a baseline against which to interpret later developments. The present chapter is mainly based on the publications of Audry Richards (1939, 1940, 1956). Although these publications are rather old, they are not obsolete. Most of the customs and values described are still common.

3.1. Traditional Bemba society

In pre-colonial times, especially in the 17th century, the Bemba formed a centralised state, based on the pre-eminence of the royal Crocodile clan, who provided the Bemba king. Succession to this high office was determined by position in the genealogy which related members of the royal clan to the ruling line, but only in conjunction with the holding of some subordinate chiefships. The kings were outstanding figures in the Crocodile clan, as well as qualified by matrilineal descent from a line of predecessors (Richards 1956, 36-42). All powerful political positions were held by the Crocodile clan, although some village headmen were commoners. The Bemba state depended on military success and the extraction of tribute and slaves from dominated peoples. Power lay in the ability to command the services of other peoples. The Bemba recognised the right to command exercised by the royal clan, but also the right of age. Children knew their position of seniority in a group (Richards 1956, 48). I noticed this also when I was living with a family in Luangwa.

Bemba women were admired among neighbouring peoples for industry in agriculture and they were famous for their independence, a measure of which is their right to plead their own cases in courts (Richards 1956, 48-49). Bemba royal women had a role in political and religious life and were in charge of ancestral shrines. Even commoner women, as the mothers of their brothers' heirs, had a position which commanded respect, and had influence which increased with age.

The Bemba are an agricultural people living for the most part in tsetse-fly country. Like the kindred matrilineal peoples such as the Bisa, Lala and Lamba, they keep practically no cattle. Their system of cultivation provides them with only a bare subsistence and they experience alternate periods of hunger and plenty every year. They are therefore unable to accumulate large stores of their staple food, which is finger millet. Next to this their main food is maize and groundnuts (Richards 1939, 20) Metal work was never highly developed and though objects like hoes and beads were exchanged in social transactions such as marriage, they were not commonly used as a currency (Richards 1940, 13). There was little storable material wealth or property. Personal possession consisted of household utensils and furniture, weapons and sacred heirlooms in noble families.

The Bemba are shifting cultivators, living in a sparsely populated area and clearing fresh strips of soil every year to plant their staple millet. Their village sites are moved every four or five years. Bemba families have the rights of use of land but no permanent ownership or claims of inheritance over it (Richards 1940, 14).

The ties uniting Bemba families and kinship groups are not property links but services, e.g. the garden work done by the son-in-law for his father-in-law, or by the subject for his chief, food and beer exchange, ritual bonds or a belief in common descent. The giving and sharing of food is an important index of social relations. The Bemba son owes his status to a member of the older generation, i.e. his maternal uncle, but he does not depend on this relative or on any other for his marriage payment. This is a difference compared to the cattle-owing Bantu, where the son depends on his father or on other male relatives, for the cattle which are to enable him to marry (Richards 1940, 14). Ties of common residence, sentiment, reciprocal services or gifts and ritual obligations have combined to unite the Bemba family as effectively as the property links binding kinsmen among the cattle-owing Bantu, although these links are more subject to variation and link a smaller group of relatives. A system of relationships mainly based on the exchange of services and the links of rituals can hardly survive in changed circumstances (Richards 1940, 15).

3.2. Marriage among the Bemba

The Bemba consider married life as the only possible existence for a man and a woman. Polygamy and the custom of inheritance of widows made spinsterhood non-existent until recently and widowhood apparently rare. Sexual intercourse is considered necessary to well-being and a pleasure to which all are entitled. More continence is expected of women than of men, but both sexes are thought to have the right to a full sex life (Richards 1940, 15). Impotence and barrenness are despised and considered sufficient grounds for divorce. Chastity in the sense of complete abstinence from sexuality is not recognised ideal at any stage of life, whether before or after marriage. The Bemba considered the prenuptial chastity demanded by the missionary as a very strange conception. Sex taboos are kept only by those passing through an abnormal state or wishing to acquire abnormal powers. Between married couples intercourse is expected to take place nightly, except during the woman's tabooed periods, and normally more than once a night (Richards 1940, 15). The sexual impulse is linked with the desire to produce and rear children for the community (Richards 1940, 18).

Among young people sexual relations are openly looked forward to and discussed, except in front of elders (Richards 1956, 50). Parents and children would never speak of sexual matters in front of each other and children above the age of weaning are not allowed to share the sleeping hut of their parents, although now required to do so by almost all the schemes of urban housing. Women frankly discuss sexual matters, but are careful of referring to these when members of different age groups are present. When I discussed the questionnaires with the women in the church lay groups, some younger members had to leave the room when we talked about sexual matters.

Among the Bemba parenthood is a basis of social status. There are no age-grades of a formal type, but men are divided into groups as married and unmarried. Married women are given status according to their children. Those past child-bearing have certain ritual privileges and duties based on this fact. Girls are divided into those who have reached puberty, which is at their menarche, and those below that age (Richards 1940, 17).

Due to these views about the importance of procreation the Bemba treat sexual intercourse in marriage as being on a different plane from that outside it. Sexual intercourse within marriage is believed to have spiritual force and can be used for the benefit of the whole community if performed in the right manner. For this reason chiefs and headmen perform special acts of intercourse as part of the ritual to bring fertility to the land or blessings on a village (Richards 1939, 25 and 1940, 18). When I was in Northern Province during the drought, I was told that the chief was to blame for the holding of the rain, because he had been unfaithful to the ancestors.

The marital relationship is thought to be subject to special dangers and is protected by specific taboos. It is thought that sex can be dangerous unless it is surrounded by certain rituals; sexual intercourse can produce physical illness or disaster unless the necessary care is taken. People who have recently engaged in sexual intercourse pass into a particular condition described as "hot". In this stage it is dangerous for them to approach the ancestral spirits, and the chief or headman has to be purified, otherwise he risks bringing disaster on his district (Richards 1940, 19 and 1956, 30). All adults are likely to be "hot" and it is dangerous for a couple not yet purified after sexual intercourse to approach their fire-place, for a fire polluted in this way may bring illness to anyone who eats the food that is cooked on it. The peril is particularly great in the case of children. Thus, parents who do not take the necessary ritual precautions may bring illness to their own children.

To remove the dangers of sex a special ceremony is required and this is one which can only be performed by a legally married couple. At marriage each girl is presented by her paternal aunt with a pot which must be treated with the utmost secrecy. With this pot the purification rite is carried out. It is filled with water and placed on the fire, husband and wife each holding the rim. Water from the pot is then poured by the wife on to her husbands hands, and some say on to the wife's as well. This ritual is the essential act which removes the condition of hotness from the body of husband and wife (Richards 1956, 31). This rite has to be performed after each sexual act and can be seen as intimacy between the spouses. The Catholic church was strongly opposed to it. Now some Bemba people also say that it is pagan to perform this ritual.

The ritual cleaning is related to the view that women are symbolically cold and related to the cold season, while men are symbolically hot and related to the hot, dry season. This combination is related to fertility. Marital sex is the interaction of the three seasons; the cold body of the woman is ready to receive the sacred gift of parenthood, from the hot influence of the man (Hinfelaar 1989, 4). For men, getting in contact with God (Lesa), or the ancestral spirits, is possible through sexual intercourse with his wife (Douglas 1966, 157; Hinfelaar 1989, 5; Richards 1956, 155).

When a woman is having her period, she is in the "cold world". This is also a dangerous stage. In this stage she is vulnerable to different kinds of danger, but even more she is considered to be dangerous herself, because she is thought to cause illness to people who are vulnerable. This means, that it is dangerous for her to have sexual intercourse, to cook or to come close to children who are not hers, because they can get ill. My informants said that many people were ill, because "women do not cook properly. They spoil their chests". They meant that women, while having their monthly period, were using salt when they were cooking. According to the tradition, women should not add salt then. Salt weakens the body, and while menstruating the body is weak already. Also salt gives sexual appetite, while no sexual intercourse is allowed during the monthly period. A woman should leave the door of her house open at night, to indicate that she is unclean and should not be touched by her husband. In the past women were not even allowed to cook when they were having their monthly period. In the Northern Province people told me that they still not cook and ask relatives or neighbours to cook for them. In the urban area however, they said it depends on the husband. If he keeps the tradition, he will cook himself or ask others to cook, but most women cook while having their period. Thus in the urban area there is less meaning given to fire, but more to salt. A woman is also unclean when she has just delivered. In the past she was not supposed to have sexual intercourse while her child was not weaned yet, because the first child would become ill if the mother became pregnant soon after delivery.

The ritual links uniting a married couple are thus particularly strong. Husband and wife perpetually carry out the dangerous act of sex together, and thereby put themselves in each other's power and depend on each other for ritual purification. To contract a marital union for the first time is dangerous. The first intercourse with a girl after her initiation rite has been performed is considered to be a perilous act and is carried out with special ritual precautions (Richards 1940, 20). In this act the ritual relationship between husband and wife is valued. The bride is given her marriage pot and thenceforth her fortunes are indissolubly linked with those of her husband. Any sexual irregularity on the part of one partner affects the other and also the children of the union, for illicit intercourse cannot be followed by the purification that is possible between legal partners. A man who commits adultery may cause his wife to be struck by various illnesses, and a woman can cause her husband to suffer. Either of them may bring death or severe illness on their children.

Worse penalties fall on a pregnant woman who has committed adultery while carrying her child, or whose husband has been unfaithful to her during that time. If the woman has committed adultery she is expected to die in childbirth (*ncentu*) unless she admits the name of her lover in time for medicine to be found to save her. If a man takes a lover while his wife is pregnant she will die after childbirth (*ncila*) unless he confesses his guilt. In these cases adultery is seen as killing the child or the wife. This is called *ukucilo mukashi*, "to step over one's spirit", and also "to mix blood". Thus blood and spirit are connected.

The ritual link between husband and wife is very close and therefore the spirit of the one is thought to linger round the body of the other. If either partner dies a relative of the same sex must sleep with the survivor to fetch back the spirit of the dead, "to take the death off" that person, otherwise the surviving spouse would be in the "cold" world with the deceased. This ritual cleansing is called *ubupiani*. Usually the relatives of the longest living take some belongings of the deceased. This is part of the inheritance system, which consists of two phases. One is the renaming of a (new born) child after a relative who has died, the second is the ritual cleansing of the longest living spouse.

Thus the Bemba conception of sex involves the recognition of physiological facts of intercourse and procreation and magic potency of the sexual act and the belief that improper sexuality brings dangers of supernatural punishment. This concept links together husband and wife in ritual interdependence, and underlies the whole Bemba system of belief in supernatural powers of fire, water and the forest, which forms the basis of political authority, since the chief is thought to control the fertility of the land through the magic influence of his virility (Richards 1940, 21). Sexuality must therefore be ordered and marriage and procreation are made the basis of social status. The Bemba sex ritual is an integral part of the old marriage contract which implied notions of the marriage relationship, parenthood and political status. Missionaries were bound to attack the Bemba notions of sexuality.

3.3. Kinship structure

Like many peoples of the Central African Plateau the Bemba have a matrilineal system and originally practised matrilocality. The household consisted of the extended family.

Men were dominant and had authority in public, e.g. chiefs were men, while women had to show respect to men (Richards 1956, 50). However, women had a high status. They were wanted because they provided the clan with new men. They were also desired for processing food, small scale industry and bearing and rearing children. They were loyal to each other and respectful to elder women (Richards 1956, 48-50).

Because of the matrilineal system women often hold high position by virtue of lineage. Before Independence (1964) they may wield political authority as chieftainesses or heads of village or hereditary guardians of shrines. The custom of matrilocal marriage gives them a strong position in village life, and as they grow older they acquire great influence in family councils and often carry out important negotiations on behalf of their sons or other male relatives. When past child-bearing a woman is socially equal to a man, can talk her mind freely before him and has a number of ritual duties and privileges.

A of lack of intimacy between the two sexes makes the ideal of companionship impossible in marriage. This is not in contradiction with the strong ritual bonds between husband and wife, but a paradox. Boys and girls are separated in early life. The two genders eat and play apart throughout adult life. There is no period of courtship but merely a proposal of marriage following the lines of a family decision. After marriage, the Bemba couple has no independent existence as an economic unit during the first years of married life. The woman continues to work and talk with her mother, sisters and other female relatives, while the husband eats and works with the other men. The two share a house at night and for the first years of married life this is the limit of their intimacy (Richards 1940, 23). During the first year after the wedding ceremony, a wife does not cook for her husband, but the mother-in-law offers him food. Today this custom is not practised anymore, due do neo-local residence and town-life. The offering of food by the woman to the man is an essential obligation of social ties. It is a duty of a wife to cook for her husband and hence it becomes a privilege (Richards 1939, 129). The husband is not allowed to speak to his mother-in-law during the first few years, as a sign of respect to her. When the couple has three or four children, the ceremony of the acceptance of the son-in-law and the daughter-in-law (*kwingisha shifyala*) takes place. Only after this ceremony is the husband allowed to speak to his mother-in-law. He has then proven to be a good husband, while the wife has proven to be a real woman by bearing some children. After this ceremony, the husband can choose in which village he wants to live (Richards 1956, 42; Epstein 1981, 68). However, marriages often remained matrilocal (Richards 1940, 28).

The ideal wife should be hard-working, a good hostess and obedient to her husband. A good husband should make big gardens for his wife and provide for her and her children, he should be patient and not beat his wife without reason. The Bemba do not expect a happy companionship in marriage (Richards 1940, 22). Affection often grows between married people, but the pattern of married relations is one of economic and sexual partnership, not of close companionship. Strong attachments of one woman to one man are often regarded as due to witchcraft. Richards (1940, 22) states that jalousies divided village life.

Children belong to their mother's clan. The lineage group is the kinship unit, of which they can claim support. The male head of this unit has rights to control the children. When a girl is about to be married, her mother's brother must be consulted and he should be given part of the marriage payment. In case of divorce he or the father is responsible for the welfare of the girl. If there are any children, the women's' people are their legal guardians and can claim possessions of the children. Although the Bemba father is and was the head of the household, his wife's people claimed considerable rights over his children (Richards 1940, 33).

3.4. Education of girls

The socialisation of a girl is a long process, which reaches its climax in the initiation rite. A young girl helps her mother with the housekeeping like sweeping, fetching water, working in the fields and looking after younger children. Thus she knows all these things, but she is not fully responsible for them.

Small girls and boys play at marriage, they build themselves tiny huts, cook, and sometimes imitate the sexual act (Richards 1940, 15). At about the age of eight the two sexes are separated at their games and no sex play is allowed any more. Probably intercourse took place secretly in the past. Adults deny this, and if it happens now, they condemn it. Pregnancy could easily be avoided while these girls had not yet started menstruating, and could also be avoided by using herbs to prevent pregnancies, which could be found in the bush. Parents used to give their daughters to their husbands before the age of puberty. Thus most girls have prenuptial intercourse with their future husbands and it must have been rare for them to reach puberty without the knowledge of or practise of sexual relations (Richards 1940, 16). Yet there is thought to be a difference between nuptial and pre-nuptial sexuality (see par. 3.2.).

When a girl is about eight to ten years old, an older woman, usually her grandmother, will teach her to extend her labia minora. Girls sometimes meet together in the bush to practise this custom. Women say the extended labia are to please their husbands but they seem to be proud of their prolonged labia. Perhaps there is a relationship between the matrilineal system and the importance of the labia.

Older women will keep an eye on the girl and tell her that she should behave properly, obey older people and dress properly. Women will take care of her not hiding with boys. This is to avoid her getting pregnant. Becoming pregnant before being initiated is thought to be a bad omen. The new born child would bring evil; it could destroy the crops and bring damage to a family and even the whole community. Being pregnant before initiation means the breaking of the ancestral law, which stipulated that only after initiation a girl is entitled to bear children and children can only be born in marriage. Nowadays there is also the fear of AIDS and other sexually transmitted diseases.

A girl's first period is solemnised by a rite in which she is doctored with medicine, ritually separated from fire and brought in contact with it again, and taught the dangers associated with menstruation (Richards 1940, 17). The initiation ceremony used to follow soon after this. It involved teaching for about six months, but now it has decreased to about three days. In chapter five I will discuss the initiation rites. The wedding ceremony followed soon after the initiation ceremony. The time between these two ceremonies was usually between one week and six months (cf. Richards 1956). In my research I noticed that the women who were born before 1960 had their wedding ceremony a few months after the initiation rites and the ones who were born in the 1960s and 70s had an average of two years between the two ceremonies. The reasons for this extended period are the prolonged schooling for girls and free education, and the changed ideas about marriage. Usually in the first year after the wedding the woman gave birth to her first child.

Fathers and daughters keep a distance between each other. Even when a girl is born, the mother will cover the abdomen of the girl before showing her to her father. Fathers and daughters are supposed to stay at a distance all their life. However, in the church lay groups the sexual abuse of girls by their fathers was often discussed. It should be remarked here, that any person has many fathers in this classificatory kinship system. Also because of the insecurity of conjugal ties of adult mothers, many girls are confronted with the presence of their mother's man, who is not a biological or formal kinship father and therefore may take liberties with her. But still it is very bad for a mother and daughter to have the same man, as they say "you do not sleep in the same bed as your mother".

For both men and women it is important to have many children. Children give them status, and for men having children means founding a house, and this gives him the right to approach his matrilineal ancestors. Thus children are important, not only for labour, but also for the survival of the clan. They are a facet of the chain of life and kinship. Therefore every grown-up is obliged to procreate (Mbiti 1990, 130). Kinship links all relatives, including the ones who have died or who are yet to be born. Therefore, it is important for children to know their ancestors. For children who are born out of wedlock, it can be bad if their father and hence their ancestors are unknown. The father sometimes wants to acknowledge his children after some time, because if he does not, he cannot be a good ancestor. A woman who does not have children is not regarded as a real woman. She can not be a good ancestor and she is the end of the chain of kinship. She is sometimes accused of being a witch and when she dies she will be buried at a cross-road, because she cannot be with her relatives who have died already. Cross-roads are dangerous places, places of evil. Although it is known that it is not always the woman's fault because her husband can be infertile, it is she who will be blamed. In this case, the man will often take another wife. Usually the woman is sent back to her parents and the couple will divorce. Because children are important for the clan and the community, all adults can help with rearing children, although the parents, particularly the mother, have the main responsibility.

3.5. Aspects of change

The processes of religious change began to emerge centuries before colonial rule (Van Binsbergen 1981, 179). For many years Zambian societies were invaded by groups aspiring to establish themselves as rulers. This caused rivalry among the priestly territorial cults in their political functions (Van Binsbergen 1981, 125).

Some types of economic link between the members of a kinship group, such as ownership of land or patriarchal authority, can be maintained fairly easy within the changed economic situation, while others are likely to disappear, and with them the solidarity of the group united by this means. The matrilocal family group of the Bemba is less readily adapted to the new economic situation than the patrilocal, patriarchal units of some of the neighbouring peoples (Richards 1940, 10). In every society the interests of some sections of the society inevitably conflict with those of others, and some individual social relationships produce strains. In a strained situation in the traditional structure, migratory labour could offer a chance of escape with the consequent weakening of kinship obligations (Richards 1940, 11).

New conditions may intensify strains that already exist, and they may create new situations of tension; conflicts between old and new allegiances (Richards 1940, 11). These conditions were the coming of Christianity to Zambia, the colonial influence that favoured the patrilineal system, the expansion of capitalism, the changed economic situation and the migration to and the grow of the towns. These factors are making for the loosening of kinship bonds and facilitate disruption in a sometimes already divided authority in the original family system.

Now that the central themes of Bemba culture have been described, I will discuss the initiation rite, which is an important factor in the lives of women. In the next chapter I will outline the general aspects of initiation rites or rites of passage, and in chapter five I will focus on the initiation rite I attended.

Initiation Rites

4

Almost every society has rituals to mark the passing of a stage in the life of an individual (cf. Van Gennep 1909). The *rite de passage* or initiation rite marks the transition from childhood to adulthood. The child passes through the stage of being a non-person to that of being a person who can take her responsibility in the community.

In this chapter I will describe initiation rites or rites of passage. First I will discuss the structure of these rites, which is more or less the same in many societies in different parts of the world (cf. Van Gennep 1909), after which I will describe these rites as they are performed in Central Africa.

4.1. The overall structure of initiation rites

All rituals, including initiation rituals, are events with a social meaning and symbolic actions (La Fontaine 1986, 11). The function of rituals is to confirm the structure of the society. Through rituals conflicts within society are made clear and may be solved. A ritual is a comment on the society (Turner 1981, 578). There is a notion of power in rites (Mauss 1972, 99). Power is ascribed to sacrificed objects and to the people performing the rites.

Initiation rites or rites of passage are transition rituals. This class comprises a variety of rites accompanying the crossing of boundaries, changes in time and in social status. All initiation rites, such as the installation of a king, or the passage from unmarried to married, have similar characteristics. The rites can be performed either individually or in a group. Rites of passage usually go together with biological changes, for girls often the onset of menstruation (La Fontaine 1986, 109) or the growing of breasts (Turner 1967, 20; Vuyk 1990, 51). These biological changes are thought to need ritual treatment.

As Van Gennep (1909, 94-96) has noticed, physiological puberty and "social puberty" are different matters, which rarely come together at the same time. Physical puberty is marked particularly by the onset of menstruation. It seems to be easy to date this as the passage from childhood to adulthood but in social life it is different. Therefore it is better to speak of initiation rites instead of puberty rites.

According to Van Gennep (1909) boundaries are considered to be dangerous. Therefore the boundaries of territories and villages are often marked by shrines and people will make offerings at the shrines to protect themselves before crossing the boundaries. Similarly, society is made up of a series of social boundaries between categories so that the social life of individuals can be seen as a series of transitions as individuals change their status. Events such as births, marriages and deaths involve the potential for danger to those in transition. The rituals of transition both mark the changes and protect the individuals concerned. The danger of such changes derives from the sanctity of all social acts. What is sacred is also dangerous and must be dealt with ritually (Van Gennep 1909).

As in every initiation rite there are three phases in the *rite de passage*: the phase of separation, the marginal phase and the phase of aggregation (Van Gennep 1909, 131, 133, 136). Turner (1967; 1969) elaborates these phases.

The first phase, the separation, comprises the symbolic behaviour signifying the detachment of the individual from an earlier phase in the social community or structure. During the intervening phase, the marginal period, which Turner (1967, 93) calls the liminal phase, the characteristics of the ritual subject or initiate are ambiguous; the initiate passes through a cultural realm that has none of the attributes of the past or the coming state. In the third phase, the aggregation, the passage is consummated. The individual or ritual subject is in a relatively stable state once more and, by virtue of this, has rights and obligations vis-à-vis others of a clearly, defined and structured type. The initiate is accepted and expected to behave according to customary norms and ethical standards.

The three forms of rituals of transition dramatise the transition by creating a margin, a boundary between the two states concerned and transforming the individual across from one to the other.

All stages have their own rituals and symbols. Often mutilation of the body is used (Van Gennep 1909, 106). The crossing of streams or other obstacles indicate separation, while anointing with medicine, eating and dressing in new clothes are integrative actions.

Liminality is marked by the invisibility of the initiate, which means that she is hidden or geographically separated, but also in many parts of the initiation rite there are phases of liminality. Because the liminal phase is the longest and most important one, I will discuss this.

The liminal phase

The liminal phase is ambiguous, because in this phase the person slips through the network of classifications that locate his or her state and position. Liminal entities are betwixt and between the positions given by law, custom, convention and ceremony. Their ambiguous and indeterminate attributes are expressed through various symbols in many societies that ritualise social transitions. Thus, liminality is linked to death, to being in the womb, to invisibility, to darkness, to bisexuality and to the wilderness (Turner 1969, 95). Liminal entities, such as the girl in the initiation rites, may be represented as possessing nothing. She is naked or wears only a slip of clothing to demonstrate that she has no status or property. Her nakedness also serves to humiliate her, for she is a non-person; she should be teased and treated badly, in order to make her strong to bear all the disappointments and pains that she will experience in life. The near nakedness is also a sign of respect to the ancestors, because it refers to a specific local part where clothing in textile was equivalent to wealth, and cloth normally came from long distance trade. The behaviour of the girl is passive and humble: she must obey her instructors and accept arbitrary punishment without complaint. Initiations with a long period of seclusion often have a rich proliferation of liminal symbols. The liminal phase blends lowliness and sacredness.

Turner (1969, 96) notes that the rites represent "a moment in and out of time and in and out of secular social structure" which reveals a recognition of a generalised social bond that has ceased to be and has yet to be divided into various structural ties. These structural ties are relationships between people and their hierarchy in society. Liminality implies that the high could not be high unless the low existed, and he who is high must experience what it is like to be low. Social life involves experiences of high and low and of equality and inequality. The passage from lower to higher status is through a limbo of statuslessness (Turner 1969, 97).

The phase of liminality is also a test which the initiate has to undergo in order to become a full member of the society. The initiate has to do things she will never again do in her life. These are symbolic actions. She has to learn particular things and when she has learned or done these things, she is taken out of the liminal phase. After the period of liminality, the initiate will get a higher status. It is like giving recognition to an essential bond, without which there could be no society (Turner 1967, 99; 1969, 97).

The girl in liminality must be a *tabula rasa*, a blank slate, on which is inscribed the knowledge and wisdom of the group or society in those respects that pertain to the new status (Turner 1969, 103). The ordeals and humiliations, often of a physiological and psychological character to which the initiate is submitted, partly represent a destruction of the previous status and partly a tempering of the essence in order to prepare the girl to cope with her new responsibilities and restrain her in advance from abusing her new privileges.

Other characteristics of liminality are submissiveness and silence. In the initiation rites the subject has to submit to an authority that represents the whole community, the repository of the culture's values, norms, attitudes, sentiments and relationships. Its representatives in the initiation rites represent the generic authority of the tradition. In tribal societies speech is not only communication, but also power and wisdom. The wisdom imparted in liminality is not just an aggregation of words but has an ontological value; it refashions the being of the initiate. Therefore the initiate is not allowed to speak. Silence is also imposed because a subject in liminality is regarded as an unborn baby, which is speechless.

Another aspect of liminality is sexuality. The resumption of sexual relations is usually a ceremonial mark of the return to society This is a feature of many societies, but in a society that strongly stresses kinship as the basis of many types of group affiliation, sexual continence has additional spiritual force (Turner 1969, 104). For kinship, or relations shaped by the idiom of kinship, is one of the main factors in structural differentiation. The undifferentiated character of liminality is reflected by the absence of marked sexual polarity.

The chastening function of liminality is a component in all initiation rites. The pedagogics of liminality represent a condemnation of two kinds of separation from the generic bond of communitas. (Turner (1969, 96) uses the word communitas not as a synonym for society, but to indicate a sort of modality of social relationship.) The first kind is to act only in terms of the rights conferred on someone by the incumbency of office in social structure. The second is to follow psychobiological urges at the expense of one's fellows. A mystical character is assigned to the sentiment of human kindness in liminality, and often this stage of transition is connected with beliefs in protective and punitive powers (Turner 1969, 105).

Liminal situations and roles are attributed with magico-religious properties and often regarded as dangerous and polluting, because in this phase people are not a part of the structure but part of "communitas", and all manifestations of communitas are dangerous and are surrounded by prohibitions and prescriptions (Turner 1967, 96). According to Douglas (1966, 122) everything that cannot be classified in terms of traditional criteria or classifications, or that fall between boundaries, is regarded as polluting and dangerous. People in liminality cannot be classified, as they are in between two classifications. Thus the initiate is polluted, which is symbolised by the covering of the initiate under a blanket and the sitting in a corner of a room or a special hut.

Thus, liminality is an interstructural phase, in which the girl is in transition, so that she gets a chance to pass the boundary which leads to a new state of life in the community. It is the first step in her life, a life in which she is grown-up, and in which she will be fully part of the community, with her responsibilities, in which she can become a mother herself and teach children.

Ritual as social action

Ritual is a special type of action; its performance requires the organised co-operation of individuals, directed by a leader or leaders. There are rules indicating which persons should participate and on what occasions; often the rules excluding certain categories of people are just as significant as those that permit or require others to take part (La Fontaine 1986, 11).

Initiation rites are mostly hidden or concealed as secret, while the last part is a public phase. This is the "coming out" into the open which is necessary to confirm the new status of the initiate. The whole ceremony in itself is regarded as a self-contained and closed entity that could hardly bear changes and modifications coming from outside.

Ritual is also social in that there is a general recognition of a correct, morally right pattern that should be followed. While changes in ritual procedure do occur, coincidentally or, on a long term base, to adapt to changes in the organisation of society, there is generally a view that ritual has a fixed structure. Although they vary from occasion to occasion, they will be judged to be more or less close to what the ideal form is believed to be. But still there is a component of spontaneity in most rituals, which responds to actual circumstances (Turner 1981, 560).

Ritual is the expression of ideas and of social meaning and an effective action. It is expected to produce results. The performance is not an end in itself but a means to achieve other ends. Initiation rites have dramatic moments, of excitement and tension, of solemnity, and also of comedy as well as an element of entertainment.

Social relationships are expressed in the organisation of ritual. The allocation of roles in the performance and the identity of those directing it are modelled on the structure of the society involved. Ritual occasions mobilise this structure in action.

La Fontaine (1986, 104) states that initiation rites are for those already initiated as much as for the novice and are thus for all participants. The human beings who perform the rituals and those who are the rituals' objects are themselves performers in a morality play; the actors stand for something other than themselves (La Fontaine 1986, 104). The acts demonstrate the relationship between the roles they occupy, which are senior and junior and society is ordered in this manner. Senior and junior form a part of the universe of meanings. The whole set of ideas evoked in ritual is the traditional knowledge of a society.

The knowledge which is revealed is claimed to be secret. However, the secrecy may be a generally maintained fiction. All initiations pass knowledge and powers that are exclusive to the initiated. It is the knowledge that others do not know. This creates a barrier between people. The knowledge has to be passed on to other generations which, of course, makes this "secret" a widely shared form of knowledge which has to be continued. This can be done by performing the ritual (La Fontaine 1986, 104).

There are common symbolic themes and an emphasis on mysterious knowledge in initiation rites, mainly based on the fact that uninitiated do not have this knowledge and do not understand the language used or taught in the ritual.

The rites also contain ideas of hierarchical order, for the initiates are not only transformed but they gain a higher status. The girls become women, although they are still not real women because they have not reached that status and have not yet given birth. Initiation is the first step to womanhood. The initiate is contrasted with the higher rank of the ones who initiate her. Their superiority is based on their greater ritual knowledge and the initiate is made to feel ignorant and confused: this serves to underline her inferiority.

Female initiation is related to post-marital residence and the contribution of female labour to the economy. It establishes adult identity and thus distinguishes between the generations (La Fontaine 1986, 108).

Initiation rites claim a fundamental distinction between male and female (La Fontaine 1986, 117). The concepts of man and woman are constructed and justified by reference to the norms emphasised by the society concerned. Sexual identity is an important aspect of adult status in all societies and the allocation of social roles to men and women is everywhere explained and justified by reference to ideas concerning their nature. In all societies there is a division of labour based on gender. In societies which lack a complex social organisation the sexual division of labour has greater importance.

The association of initiation with organisation based on descent indicates that sexual identity is likely to be a key concept in understanding it (La Fontaine 1986, 117). Maturity rituals are usually dramatic reinforcements of sexual distinctions, designed to underline the separation between the genders. They are concerned with affirming adult status in terms of the opposed categories of gender. Sexual identity is public and cannot be separated from the individual's other social roles (La Fontaine 1986, 118).

The social division by gender may imply complementarity but it implies asymmetry as well. Usually the ideas associated with masculinity are superior, at least in the inter-gender discourse. Thus, the ritual that marks the division of the sexes also produces the justification for a male domination in society, even in those societies where descent is reckoned through women and only women are initiated. Rites of passage are normally mandatory: all individuals must go through them. It is not a matter of choice (La Fontaine 1986, 103).

Power and authority

Rituals exist to confirm the power of certain people (Mauss 1972, 99; La Fontaine 1986, 116). In initiation rite the superiority of older people and the power and authority of the ones who perform the rite in particular are shown.

Knowledge is often related to power. Usually power and authority are associated, for power is legitimatised by an appeal to moral principles and authority gives access to economic and political power. Authority is the recognised right to command, legitimatised by appeal to principles which are part of the moral order. Authority is also related to status. Status is a form of office. Office needs a mandate from society given through its responsible institutions, making it legitimate.

The legitimacy of ritual teachers is that of traditional knowledge. The information, understanding and experience is needed to ensure the correct performance. La Fontaine (1986, 32) claims that the structure of authority is important. Ranking by order of accession to adult status and a notion of the collective wisdom of experienced seniors is produced by performing regular initiation rites. The legitimate authority of seniors may not coincide with the distribution of effective power which may be exercised mainly by holders of office or by self made leaders.

Ritual is also concerned with legitimacy, reaffirming the divisions and hierarchy that are indispensable to a system of authority. The ones who conduct a ritual can also be given fees for specialist services.

The transformation of individuals, by the ritual which transfers them from one state to another, is a demonstration of the power of ritual knowledge. The individuals are objects used in the ritual, rather than its central focus through which the ritual is to be explained (La Fontaine 1986, 33).

The women who conduct the initiation are accepting serious responsibilities and a successful outcome tests qualities in the initiators as well as in the initiates (La Fontaine 1986, 114). The women always make sure that the girl passes all the tests and ordeals. If she fails the first time, she has to try again, until she passes. If she were to fail, her mother could be blamed as well as the one who teaches, because people could doubt her skill.

Symbolic meaning: passing the boundary

Ritual acts are symbolic; they express significant social ideas by associating the physical with the social. In social life there is a set of ideas concerning the divisions of categories. By regulating the relation of individual events to the basic divisions, the social order and boundaries are maintained. The ritual transfer of individuals across them is the means by which they are made manifest and reaffirmed as significant.

Ritual mobilises authority behind the granting of office and status and thus guarantees the legitimacy and imposes accountability for its proper exercise. The same distinction between individuals and their roles is made in initiation. The experience of initiation is identified as conferring on the initiate knowledge or rights which underline and justify an increase in status, which is publicly acknowledged. The rights acquired in initiation also entail duties, as is often the case in traditional societies (Richards 1956, 187). One of these duties is the obedience to senior people. The status of the initiates is linked to the experience of what they have undergone and what is revealed to them. This implies that the people of higher status have further knowledge and greater power (La Fontaine 1986, 104).

Much of the ritual knowledge consists of rules of what is to be done and the materials to be used. Regular participation in rituals may transfer much of this information so that experienced participants can direct rituals on their own responsibility. Also much of the understanding depends on impression and association, on experience in the daily world and its social relationships. Ritual expresses concepts and ideas which order experience and give moral authority to the ideal form of social relationships, but experience also informs one's understanding of ritual as it is performed (La Fontaine 1986, 103).

The contrast with the normal social order emphasises and manifests the boundaries which the rites serve to create. Initiation rites emphasise this boundary, between young and old, male and female, and give the right to pass the boundary.

4.2. Initiation rites for girls in Central Africa

There are many similarities in the initiation rites in Central Africa, although there are also differences.

Richards (1956) noticed that in Zambia, Bemba girls experience puberty rituals individually at their first menstruation. These rituals are a necessary preliminary to initiation, which is performed later, when several girls undergo it together. The girls are kept inside until the bleeding stops, because it is believed that the blood is dangerous, particularly to children. White *et al.* (1958, 206) claim that among the Luvale, another group in Central Africa, blood is symbolically associated with life and fertility rather than with danger. During initiation, it is prohibited for a girl to have contact with fire in order to avoid prolonged menstruation or to avert sudden deaths in the village. The Luvale have no special ceremonies required to remove dangers believed to be inherent in sexual intercourse (White *et al.* 1958, 205). For the Bemba the three elements blood, sex and fire combine to present constant dangers, for the Luvale they are associated with limited and specific dangers on certain occasions only (White *et al.* 1958, 206). In the Luvale rites the onset of menstruation is accompanied by a strict taboo on eating and drinking. The initiate is given medicines to ensure an easy menstruation after which the ban on eating is removed (White *et al.* 1958, 208).

For the Gisa, another people in Central Africa, the onset of menstruation is also the sign of puberty and the reason to perform the initiation rite. The girl must keep food taboos. For a Gisa woman maturation is marked by three rites of passage: at her first menstruation; her marriage; and when she bears her first child (La Fontaine 1972, 163). A Gisa woman is subjected to the ancestors of her natal lineage all their life; she is not, unlike the women of other patrilineal societies, transferred to the aegis of her husband. Blood is associated with wounds and death, but also with life. Blood flowing from the female genitals is powerful in that it is associated with the natural power of women, their inherent physiological qualities of child-bearing. It is dangerous, both for the women and others. A menstruating woman must refrain from many activities lest she spoils them (La Fontaine 1972, 164). Among the Ndembu, however, the rite is performed when the girl's breasts begin to ripen (Turner 1967, 20). Here the ritual is centred around a tree which symbolises the tie of nurturing between mother and child, breast feeding, matrilineality, the unity and continuity of the Ndembu society (Turner 1967, 21).

In pre-colonial times initiation rites in South Central Africa took from two to six months, in which time the girl learned many things about the world of the ancestors, sexuality, motherhood, herbs, medicine and the working in the fields. Often marriage is an important topic in initiation rites. The ritual brings together in action human beings whose organised activity demonstrates the power of the community and of experience required through living in it (La Fontaine 1986, 78).

There is a relation between initiation rites and the organisation of the descent group. Among the Bemba the contradiction between "the masterful male and the submissive son-in-law", and between "the young woman backed by her own relatives and the submissive wife" finds expression in the initiation rite, *chisungu*, which might be regarded as an expression of the dilemma of a matrilineal society in which men are dominant but the line goes through the woman (Richards 1956, 50).

4.3. *Chisungu* and the matrilineal system of the Bemba

Richards (1956, 36-43) points to a connection with a system of chiefly authority and social structure which combined the tracing of descent through women with placing the control of domestic and political groups largely in the hands of men.

In pre-colonial times the king and all political officials under him were responsible for the ritual welfare of their people. The ritual powers of the king derived from his ability to approach the royal ancestors, whose jurisdiction included all Bemba. The wives of headmen, lineage heads and chiefs, up to and including the king had the responsibility of ensuring the purity of their husbands so that the ancestral ritual might be effective (Richards 1956, 30). Royal ritual and the initiation of girls were the two major rituals of the Bemba. They were contrasting: royal ritual was secret, involved only the ones qualified by descent, and the ancestral rituals consisted largely of praying and offerings to the ancestors. Girl's initiation, *chisungu*, was public, involving many people, much singing and dancing, as well as secret symbols. There is no initiation rite for boys. They are usually thought by their grandfather and during their wedding ceremony by a *banacimbusa*. The office of *banacimbusa*, which means "mother of secrets" (Richards 1956, 59) or "mother of sacred emblems" (Corbeil 1982, 9) is not inherited but achieved by apprenticeship and learning. The two rituals are linked by their dependence on notions of purity, the maintenance of which is the responsibility of women, passed on in the *chisungu*. The symbol of this is the marriage pot, given to a girl at her marriage (see chapter three).

Social values are expressed and maintained by the ritual, that has a wider significance than impressing the initiated with the change of status. The girl herself, for whose benefit the ritual is ostensibly performed, fades into insignificance and becomes almost invisible. She is the occasion for the rite, but not the audience for its message (Richards 1956, 127).

The explicit purpose of the *chisungu* is to change a girl into a woman, by transforming her in the course of the experience. All the overt emphasis is placed on marriage, the woman's responsibilities, subservience to her husband and to senior women and all others in authority. The rituals used to be opened by the headman of the village but men play little part in them, except that the girl's betrothed or someone who stands in for him must perform certain rites (Richards 1956, 63; Corbeil 1982, 17; La Fontaine 1986, 103). No men of the descent group take part. In pre-colonial times the *chisungu* was followed by the marriage. The future husband had to pay a part of the expenses of the initiation of his betrothed.

The symbolic representation of male and female links the initiation with sex, fire and blood, and also with the structure of authority. Bemba women and the *chisungu* ritual represent rank and social continuity, while chiefs and men are symbols of the power to shape events and also to destroy, a power which is beneficial only when contained by the constraints of descent and tradition. The *chisungu* is at one level a manifestation of the interdependence of kingship and the descent groups of commoners (Richards 1956, 167).

Chiefs are expected to be generous (the Bemba have some sayings about this) and in the initiation rite men are compared with chiefs. Bemba believe that the substance of a child is entirely that of its mother (Richards 1956, 160). The role of the father is to activate his wife's fertility, which makes the comparison with a chief in his role as organiser and leader even more apposite.

The emphasis on rank and precedence, on the co-operation between clans, necessary because people are supposed to marry outside their clan, emphasises the traditional rights which pertain to people as occupiers of social ranks and members of matrilineal clans.

The knowledge to which girls are introduced is secret, is only for those who are initiated, and its significance is not explained in the rite. This knowledge and the symbols, provided by the ancestors who established the pattern of the Bemba society, are the material embodiment of tradition. Their power is directed by an individual, a *banacimbusa*, whose authority depended largely on ability and experience (Richards 1956, 167). The interdependence between hereditary rank and the ability of individuals were ideas which supported the Bemba state. The destruction of that state by the colonial power probably contributed more to the decline of the practice of female initiation than either missionary endeavour or western education (cf. Richards 1956).

In (pre)-colonial times the initiates were helpers at the following rites for other girls, and by helping, a girl could become a *banacimbusa* herself. The majority of the *banacimbusas* told me that this was the way they had become a *banacimbusa*. It is still the case that a girl can become a *banacimbusa* this way, but more often now the *banacimbusas* are related to the church, although there are still *banacimbusas* who are not related to a church. I will return to this in chapter six.

Now that there is no ritual kingship anymore, initiation has also changed. The rites used to take several months. Richards (1956, 55), who attended the rite in 1931, describes them as lasting for four weeks. She states that they were shortened and in many places they were not performed at all (Richards 1956, 139). Nowadays the rite takes three days. This is what I noticed in the urban area, but people in the villages and girls who went to the village to experience initiation rite also told me that the rite is only performed for a few days.

Despite the influence of colonial power and Christianity, initiation rites are still performed today. In the next chapter I will describe the initiation rite which I attended on the Copperbelt.

5

Initiation Rites in Women's Church Groups on the Copperbelt

In the previous chapter I have discussed initiation rites in general. In the present chapter I will describe how the initiation rite on the Copperbelt is performed today. This description is based on the initiation rite I attended, which was performed by members of the women's church group of the Nazarethi. The women who performed the rite were all said to be Bemba, except for the chairlady of this group, who was a Ngombo, but claimed to be Bemba. The women claimed the rite to be a "traditional Bemba" rite.

5.1. General aspects of girls' initiation rites on the Copperbelt

Girls' initiation rites on the Copperbelt are individual and should be performed at first menstruation. The individual initiation may be due to the more individual kind of life people lead in town.

Today the rite is performed some years after the onset of menstruation, which shows that the focus of the rite is a social rather than a biological change. It is often postponed, mainly for financial reasons. The association of the ritual with the natural event is destroyed then.

The assumption is that the girl has so far been a virgin. However, this is not so in practice. The girl is supposed to know nothing about sexuality, which is nowadays hardly ever the case. At school she learns about sexuality and many girls have sexual relationships. When girls are about ten years old, they are supposed to extend their labia. In this way they have some sexual experiences but the main thing is that they have not had sexual intercourse. They can simulate that they do not know about sexuality as long as they have not given birth (see chapter 3). The emphasis is on virginity before marriage. This underlines the difference between immature lovers and procreation, which is the privilege of married adult men and women.

People explained that the ritual should be performed with the assistance of several women because otherwise the performers might forget to teach some items so others have to help, but actually it is because the ritual is for the women who are performing the rite, so that they can remind themselves and others of what they have learned long ago. All the women who attend the rites have to participate. Participation means demonstrating membership of the community and concern for public goals. It is an affirmation of loyalty and also a test that the people in the room really have knowledge.

There is an element of entertainment, but it is no longer a happening where people and relatives who live far away can meet, as Richards describes in *Chisungu*. It is more of a private happening, with very few people attending. In the Catholic part of Luangwa initiation rites are conducted by *banacimbusas* who are members of a women's church group.

The initiation rite is basically a symbolic activity using actions, language and images to explain and affect their world-view and specifically what it means to be an adult and a married woman in the community. The emphasis is on the power and authority of senior women, but the girl is also taught about her own power and self-respect. Hygiene and jealousy are other items. Throughout the rite there is an emphasis on the need for self-reliance. The girl is taught about food taboos she has to keep. Respect for elders is also involved.

5.2. Organisational aspects of the initiation rite

The rite I attended took three days. The first day the performance was in the afternoon and evening, the second day the clay models and drawings were made during day time, and the third day the performance was during the evening and went on the whole night.

The first part of the rite took place in the bush, which was actually near the township. The second part was performed in the house, where the symbols were revealed to the girl. The third stage was outside of the house, where she was shown to the community.

The initiation took place at the house of the grandmother. Because men were not allowed, her uncle (mother's brother), who lived in the house, went for three day to his sister, who was the mother of the girl. The mother was not allowed at the rite, except for some parts. At these parts however, the classificatory mother, in casu her grandmother and sometimes her mother's sister (my interpreter) replaced the biological mother. The biological mother only came to the house when the rite was over.

The participants in the rite were eight women, which were one *banacimbusa*, one main assistant, three other assistants and three drummers, my interpreter and me. My interpreter, who was the classificatory mother, was not allowed at some parts, e.g. in the bush. Therefore she stayed at a distance.

The girl concerned was 15 years old, and had had her menarche just over a year before the initiation rite took place. She had lived together with her grandmother (mother's mother) since she was three years old, until about a year before her initiation rite. Her father had died two years ago. The girl was at school, but could take a few days of. Like many initiation rites now, her initiation rite was postponed mainly because of lack of money.

Traditionally if the girl had her first menstruation in the months of September or October the rite was postponed, because this is the hot and dry season which is bad for fertility. It is believed to be a bad omen to have a celebration during this period and it is said that people who are born or initiated (reborn) during this period, will be troublesome or ill and will not become old. Obviously, a girl is not responsible for the timing of the onset of menstruation.

Because I contributed to the costs of the food and beer, the rite was performed during my stay, in the dry season. If I would not have been there, the girl would have experienced an initiation rite at a later stage and perhaps it would have been less elaborated.

Most of the clay models which are described by Richards (1945 and 1956) and Corbeil (1982) are represented by drawings at present. There are also new images and others have disappeared. In the house where I witnessed an initiation rite there were 34 drawings on the wall and 7 clay models. *Mbusa* refers both to the clay models and the drawings. To make it more clear, I use the word "drawings" for the drawings on the wall, and *mbusa* for the clay models.

In the two weeks afterwards the girl went to school, and in the afternoon, she had to see the *banacimbusa* to learn about the drawings. During this time the clay models were not explained, because they were destroyed immediately after the rite.

The drawings and claymodels were explained to me by the *banacimbusa* and my interpreter during the rite. Afterwards I spoke to the *banacimbusa* several times to check the information. In the next sections I will describe the rite chronologically.

Preparation for the initiation rite
The initiation rite that I witnessed was organised by the grandmother of the girl and her uncle, mother's brother. As they were Catholics, they wanted the girl to be initiated by Catholic women.

The grandmother was a chairlady of the Legio, but because there was some tension in this group, she decided to ask the Nazarethi, who specialises in initiation rites. In this group there was one woman in particular who she wanted to be the *banacimbusa* of her granddaughter. This woman had to ask permission from the chairlady of the Nazarethi, as a sign of respect to the chairlady, who is a *banacimbusa* herself. She is higher in the hierarchy, because she is a chairlady.

About two weeks before the initiation rite started, negotiations began between the grandmother and the *banacimbusa*, and later between the grandmother and all the *banacimbusa* in the Nazarethi. The negotiations were about the amount that should be paid in cash and beer, and even during the initiation rite the negotiations went on. Food and beer are used to fulfil all sorts of social obligations, to reward labour or to honour people of position (Richards 1939, 109). At first, the *banacimbusa* and her helpers, all members of the Nazarethi, said they would not ask a large amount of money because they are Christians. They knew they would be paid. However, during the ceremony they were asking for more money, beer and food. They were saying that the grandmother would not be able to pay all this. It looked as if they were saying that the grandmother was not able to pay a proper amount for the important job they were doing.

There were also negotiations between the grandmother and the husband of the *banacimbusa*. They said this was because she has to be out for one night, so they have to ask permission, and also because she has to bring in a certain amount of money or presents, and the husband should know about that. But there is another reason: the *banacimbusa* is the one who introduces the girl to the women's world and teaches her about sexuality, so actually she takes the place of a man (the future husband).

After a week they agreed that the initiation rite would start at Wednesday, which was the last day in September, and finish on Saturday morning. Often initiation rites have their last and most important day during the weekend. However, as they were Catholics, they wanted it to finish on Saturday, so they could go to church on Sunday.

The first day of the initiation rite

The initiation rite starts in the afternoon. The eight women gather around the grand-mother's house. They start talking about the way they should conduct the initiation rite.

The opening of the rite had to be done by the chairlady of the Nazarethi, because she is higher in hierarchy, so she has the honour of starting the initiation.[1]

> The *banacimbusa*, the chairlady and one helper go into a room, where they tell the girl to come. She has to undress herself, and the chairlady teaches her how to use the bandage. She gives the girl instructions about how she is supposed to behave during the initiation rite.

The girl has to be silent, to sit with her legs stretched in front of her, her hands on her legs and her head bowed. She is not allowed to do anything, and when she has to stand up, she is pulled up and put down afterwards. This makes the girl understand that she has to learn to obey and show her that she is still a child, a non-person, who cannot do anything. She has to wear a *citenge* (cloth) around her abdomen, (they call this the clothes of the initiation) so that the rest of her body is naked. This is to show that she is different from the other women. It also serves to humiliate her, to stress she is a non-person who should be teased and treated badly, in order to make her strong to bear all the disappointments and pains she will experience in life. It is also a sign of respect to the ancestors.

She is in the liminal phase, but also symbolically secluded.

> The girl has to walk behind the *banacimbusa*, while she is covered with two blankets. They enter another room, where eight women and the grandmother of the girl are waiting. The latter rolls on the floor, and dances with two plates covered with another plate.

---

[1] I illustrate my description of the initiation rite with my field-notes, which are printed in a different type

The rolling on the floor is a sign of respect for the ancestors (Richards 1956, 58). My informants told me that in this case it was also respect from the grandmother for the *banacimbusa*, who will teach her child, but also respect from the *banacimbusa* for the grandmother, who has reared the child and entrusts her to the *banacimbusa* now. It is a sign of politeness and obedience; one makes oneself humble. It is also a sign of welcome. This used to be done for a chief, and in this case the grandmother welcomes the women. In the initiation this was done many times by all the women, as a sign of respect for the ancestors.

> The grandmother puts the plates in front of the *banacimbusa*, who dances on her knees with the plates in her hands. She puts them in front of another woman, who starts dancing with the plates. One of the plates contains pumpkin pips, groundnuts and maize, the other one contains money.

My interpreter said they use pumpkin pips, groundnuts and maize because maize is the most important ingredient in the diet of the Bemba, while pumpkin and groundnuts are vegetables which are easy to grow and are symbols of fertility. In every ceremony beans are used, because this is the first relish. Beans should be given to a visitor, as a big welcome. The second relish is chicken, and this too shows that someone is welcome. They say having or giving a chicken means one will not be brought into disgrace. Also giving beans, maize, pumpkin and groundnuts will not disgrace one. Therefore they are used in the initiation rite.

The girl was not really secluded from others, only symbolically; so she was hidden under a blanket and had to sit in the corner of the room to denote that she was *nachabindwa*, taboo. She is also polluted because she is supposed to have her first menstrual period or is associated with menstrual blood.

My interpreter said that she had to be covered because otherwise bad spirits could make her face ugly. In the past the girl was covered under a blanket or veil most of the time. Only the bridegroom was allowed to take it off. In the past when someone had given birth and people asked what sex it was, they answered that it was a diamond, which means a girl. It is particularly said a girl is like a diamond when she reaches puberty. They want the diamond/grown up girl not to be seen or touched.

I think the word diamond also has a symbolic meaning, representing the vulva and associated with fertility. The covering is also because she is a non-person and has to be humiliated and humble. So this is the phase of seclusion.

> Three women are drumming, all of them are singing.

> | *Banmayo leteni ubulobo* | We are fishermen, bring your nets to catch |
> | *tulobe mpende* | a fish. We have caught a girl, we want to |
> | *mpende yakaminwa* | teach her. |

> This song means that the girl has to acquire knowledge. The girl is like a fish, who asks for knowledge and the women have to teach her.

My informants said the Bemba were originally fishermen, so this is part of their tradition. In my view it is also a sign of fertility, because a fish is associated with fertility. Richards (1939, 337) says that the one who catches a fish, is the owner. Thus this part of the ritual is done by the *banacimbusa*, who is her owner now.

While they are singing, the *banacimbusa* takes a plate and goes round with it, so that everyone can put some money on it.

One has to pay, to get the knowledge revealed. Paying is a sign of respect for the *banacimbusa* and for the culture . It is also symbolical.

Yande yande yande umwana wandi nakula	I am happy because my daughter has come of age,
yande yande nomba twaba batatu	she is mature now, now we are three.

The (grand)mother is supposed to sing this song, they argue about this.

While singing the *banacimbusa* takes the girl by twining her toes around the toes of the girl and puts her in the middle of the room. They roll on the floor, while the *banacimbusa* puts the girl's face and her own face left, right and left again on the floor, as a sign of respect.

Walomba imisango kubakulu wemwana wambusa walomba imisango kubakulu	You child of the mbusa are asking how to be an adult

This song means that the girl has to acquire knowledge, she has to learn from older, experienced people, because they have gone through this. She has to learn so that she will have a good marriage and future.

Nekambusa kanono nakutabataba nakubula mano	I am a small teacher, I do not claim to know everything.

In this song the women ask permission from the girl's grandmother to go ahead and teach the girl.

Amano yambusa mulangilemone	Teach her knowledge, teach her the facts of life

Nalomba bushe talomba kamo	The one who asks a question does not ask just one question

This means that the girl should be fully instructed.

In a prayer they say they are going to the bush because this is the way their ancestors did it, and they ask them to help them to come back safely. They end this prayer in a Catholic way, saying "In the name of the Father, the Son and the Holy Spirit, Amen".

It looks like they are used to end prayers in this way. After this, they go to the bush. The bush represents the seclusion from the community.

While going to the bush, the girl is dressed, because, as they say, they do not want others to see that there is something happening, because they might be followed. (Later on people were saying that the women were not serious, because the girl is not supposed to be dressed but should be covered and not be seen.) They take an axe, two bags containing *fitenge*, a cup, pumpkin pips, groundnuts and maize, a drum and a jerrycan with traditional beer, *kangala*.

My interpreter tells me that they are "looking for" a *mubwilili* tree, also called *cena chisungu* tree. This is the kind of tree usually used for initiation rites. It bears many fruits, so it is a symbol of fertility, meaning that the girl should bear many children. It has herbal or medical qualities, particularly for cleansing and for menstrual periods. Some said: "If the girl is menstruating again in four weeks time, then the medicine has worked. It is a "female" tree".

When they arrive at the tree, they start ululating and running around the tree, showing happiness. Every ceremony has to start with thanking the ancestors and this is the way to thank the ancestors that they have showed them the way to this tree. They act like they are hunting around the tree. My interpreter says this is to show that men hunt and women plough while they are in the bush.

They undress the girl, so that only her abdomen is covered, and put her under the tree, with her back towards it. They sing

> Umupundu shimona mukosa   Umupundu (special kind of fruit)
> mayo ee na kolele mailo   I have picked it yesterday

It is a song to honour the girl, to celebrate that she has her first period.

My interpreter says that the women are supposed to offer some beads to the ancestors, but they have forgotten to bring the beads with them. They are discussing what to do. The *banacimbusa* decides that she will use the beads she wears around her waist. She takes two white beads, which the girl, sitting on her knees with her face to the tree now, has to throw away; one to the east, representing the new life of the girl, one to the west, representing the place where the ancestors are. They sing a song, which is a prayer to the ancestral spirits, *mipashi ya ifikolwe*, saying that they are here because this is what their ancestors used to do, they are teaching the girl and asking the ancestral spirits to help them to do their job properly, to strengthen the girl during the initiation rite, to help her to keep the rules she is learning now, so that she will be a good woman, have a good husband and a good future. The *banacimbusa* ends by saying: "You taught this to our parents, and we learned this from them, so we are doing it now. We are doing this to remember you."

It shows that the ancestors are still important.

They dance while they sing a song:

> Mpeni akalonde indime akabala ee,   Give me a hoe so I can plough
> akabala kalala

One woman with the axe acts as if she is ploughing; she beats the axe on the ground, near the tree. Two women make small holes in the ground and put the pumpkin pips, beans and maize into them. One woman shows the girl how to make proper heaps of the seeds. They sing a song, saying that the girl should learn how to live with the earth, to trust in the earth and to use the earth to sow.

Then the *banacimbusa* shows her how to pick up the seeds from the soil with her mouth. When she is finished, she puts her face on the soil, left, right, left. Then the girl has to pick up the seeds, while the *banacimbusa* is holding the hands of the girl on her back. With her face on the soil, she has to eat all the seeds. The women dig with their hands in the soil under the tree where the seeds have been lying.

Ndinokusheka nshinkila *nande nshekilile* *yamulomo*	"Oh my seed, I plant you, not for you, a liar, so I put it for you liar, Oh my seed I make you ready"

My interpreter explains the song, which means that a woman is supposed to work hard, because if she does not work, she will become a beggar, and if she is a beggar she will become a liar. If she learns to work in the field, she will not have to beg, so she will not become a liar. Lying begins with begging.

In my opinion the girl does not really learn how to plough, which would be irrelevant in town. Most people do not have a field, but if her family did, then the girl would have known how to plough. It refers to the fact that she has to cook food for her family and also to show respect for the earth. It also refers to her own fertility.

To take the seeds with the mouth shows that the orifices of the body are important from now on; she has to control her speech (mouth) and vulva (virginity). Many acts in the ritual are done with the mouth. Eating with the mouth in the soil is also a sign of humility. The seeds are a symbol of fertility.

The women crawl on their backs around the tree. One woman goes first, then the girl, then the other women.

My interpreter says this is acting like a maggot. A maggot is a symbol of tidiness and activity, and not as in western society a symbol of death and decay. They sing a song which says that women have to cook and be active like a maggot.

Mwamumona nacinsebele *cita baume mu munsoli*	Be docile to your husband so that you become numerous and prosperous

The women dance around the tree, while the girl is sitting under it. Then they put the girl away from the tree. A white bracelet is hung in the tree. One of the helpers tries to take it out of the tree with her foot, while she is standing on her hands. She fails, and then the *banacimbusa* climbs the tree, while she is hanging upside down. She takes the bracelet with her toes. Then the girl has to do it. Standing on her hands, with her feet in the tree, she manages to get the bracelet with her foot out of the tree.
The white bracelet is hung back in the tree again. When the girl touches the bracelet with her toes, the women turn her, and she has to hang in the tree on her hands and feet. They sing a song: "Oh monkey, be active, like you usually are." Now she has to take the bracelet with her mouth. The women sing a song, saying that a girl should never open her legs, if someone is proposing to her, she should discuss this with her parents, and wait until the bride price is paid.

My informants said that a monkey represents activity, but also stealing, so she should not steal. The climbing in the tree is a symbol that she has grown up and can face the problems in life. The bracelet is the symbol of marriage, which should be forever and white is the colour of purity.

A woman is waving with a branch around the tree, which is, according to my interpreter, to clean it from bad spirits and to evoke the good spirits. Some of the women go to take some branches of other trees, which are called *mufungu* and *mupundu* trees. My interpreter says that these trees have sweet fruits, and are a symbol of fertility. With the branches and leaves they go back to the *mubwilili* tree. When they come back, they dig holes in the soil, while sitting on their knees and dancing with their hips. They sing:

> *Nalimwene mulume Chula ee*   "Bush pig starts to dig in the soil".
> *Nanya naikala pa cipapa*

My interpreter says this means boys are playing with boys, and girls are playing with girls. Thus it is a warning not to socialise with boys.

The girl is sitting with her back close to the tree, while they cover the girl with the branches and leaves of the *mufungu* and *mupundu* trees, which they put on her one by one. The song they sing says that the girl is not supposed to have many (female) friends, but she should choose only one. My interpreter says this is because otherwise she will not be trusted, because friends will tell each other secrets. The women are shouting, yelling, teasing the girl, calling her names, calling her a *cipelelo*, and whistling at her. They tell her never to sleep with a boy, because otherwise she will become thin and her fingers will grow long. She should hide her body. They say that men are stupid, so she has to hide from men and be careful. If she is having "slim disease" they know that she did not hide herself and has been moving carelessly.

"Slim disease" is the name for AIDS. People hardly ever speak about AIDS, but it is common to use the term "slim disease".

> *Nakumanya ciwa mu lubansa no lwendela*   I saw a ghost in the manger who visited
> you.

My interpreter says this song means that they keep her in a manger, but that she should not keep her house as a manger. This means that she should not allow men into her house, and that she is not supposed to "jump over the rules".

A house may be taken literally, but may also refer to the vagina. This reference is not only made here, but throughout South Central Africa.

They shout and take the branches away, and again they cover her with the branches. The women lift her up and put her down a few meters away from the tree.

According to my interpreter this was because the tree she was sitting under was a symbol of a house or somewhere else she felt safe, or a person. Now she has to make it on her own in the open field. The leaves she is covered with are now a symbol of the house, which means that when she is leaving the house, she is not supposed to go to men.

Then the women shout at her that she has to run. My interpreter explains that it means that she is running away from men, so she has to stay in the house/under the leaves and is not supposed to allow a man to touch her. After this she is put under the leaves again by the *banacimbusa*. Two women beat this heap with some branches and she has to run again. The women are ululating while she is running back.

Then the girl has to jump over the branches. The *banacimbusa* is standing on the other side of the heap, with her back to it. The girl jumps over the branches, on the back of the *banacimbusa*.

My interpreter compared this with jumping over a bridge or passing a border, which means that the girl is not supposed to jump over the things which they teach her: she has to put effort to keep what she learns now. If she falls or touches the branches, it would mean that she will be talking about what they teach her, although she is not allowed to do so. She also has to "jump" over boys, symbolising that when a boy wants to touch her, she has to go to the *banacimbusa*, her parents or elder people, who will protect her.

The women sing a song, because the girl has her initiation in the dry season and call her a *citongo*, a bad girl, someone who has not learnt the rules.

The women lift her up and carry her to the tree, while they hold branches for the girl's face. They put her on her knees under the tree, and make her *citenge* long so that her legs are covered. They sing: "Come you *citongo*, who grew up when it was hot and tiresome."

They sing a song to tell the girl that she should have respect for her parents and elder people and that she should help them.

Ciminine ciminine wa mwana	Stand up, stand up you child,
ciminine ena eminina pa baku ciminine	stand up so that they will stand up for you

The women are going to lay down next to the girl. They tell her that sleeping with her is a sign of respect, and that she too has to show respect.

One by one the women say who they are. One of them says she is a Bemba. Another one says she is a scorpion and sleeping outside. The next one says: "My chief is chief Chishimba". All women say their ritual names. My interpreter says that this is to introduce themselves, but also to show that they have taught the girl. They tell her to speak like them, and to choose the name of one of these *banacimbusa*. She says: "*nine Chileshe ne ka mbusa kanono*", which means: "I was taught by *Chileshe*, the great teacher, and I am a small teacher." This means that the spirit of *Chileshe* will protect her.

My interpreter explains that Chileshe is the name of the girl's grandmother on mother's side. Chief Chishimba is the royal spirit of the Bemba. A scorpion is a symbol of danger. Every *banacimbusa* has a ritual name. Here again the ancestors are important, and the women claim to be Bemba.

One by one, laying on their backs the women drink some beer which is on a plate, and is "blessed by the ancestral spirits". They creep to this plate, and in a very inconvenient way they have to drink it. Some women need help to do this. Then the girl is put on her knees under the tree. They tell her to keep the name of the *banacimbusa* (*Chileshe*) in her mind, and whenever she drinks, she should remember this name. It is the spirit of the *banacimbusa*, which she always has to bear with her.

Naobaombele kuli mayo tekuba kuchenjele *weeobaombele kuli mayo tekubula kuchenjela lelo*	The girl has to say the name of her *banacimbusa*

There is a discussion whether the girl should drink the beer on the plate. It ends up that the girl is not allowed to drink it. The chairlady does not drink, and for the others this is a sign that she "knows nothing", meaning that she has not had a proper initiation rite herself, so she is not a good *banacimbusa*. She is the only non-Bemba, she is a Ngombo from Luapula. They start quarrelling and the chairlady leaves. The *banacimbusa* is the last one who drinks from the beer. The women are singing that there is only one *banacimbusa*, and the girl should remember her name.

I was informed that the girl was not allowed to drink the beer, because otherwise she can say that these women have taught her this bad habit. Although the girl is not supposed to talk about the initiation, many girls do. However, later on I found out that the beer was an offer to the ancestral spirits. As the girl was not yet grown up - she was still a non-person - she could not make an offering to the spirits.

This also shows the division between high and low, which is carried out in the initiation. The girl is low, she is barely dressed, while the others are dressed, drinking and smoking.

My interpreter tells me that they are supposed to take medicine from the tree, to rub on the girl.

The girl is put right under the tree, while the *banacimbusa* takes some of the bark of the tree with an axe. They say if the girl does not use the medicine, her belly will swell. The women sing a song.

After this they go back to the house. While walking, the women start quarrelling. Some of them want to go on with the initiation all night, in order to finish it as soon as possible, because according to them the grandmother has not enough money to pay food and beer for three days. Some want to go on tomorrow night, others want it on Friday night, which was the agreement with the grandmother. My interpreter, the girl and I are walking ahead. We wait for the rest to come. It takes a long time, and only one of the women comes and walks with us back to the township. She is complaining about the other women, who are drunk and not serious, and saying that it is irresponsible to leave the girl in the bush while it is dark, and giving her a bad example of how to behave. "How can this girl teach others later? She will teach in a bad way, like these women."

It shows that the girl is not important, she is the occasion for the rite, not the audience for its message.

When they arrive in the township they are singing and they sing all the way to the house. They are carrying branches. When they arrive at the house of the girl's grandmother, they throw the branches on the roof of the house.

My informants say this is to denote that the girl who lives here has just reached maturity. The *banacimbusa* says that it is to make the girl fertile.

The grandmother is rolling on the floor in the house, while the women enter the house backwards.

Twingile shani ee	How do we enter the house, let us go
twingile musense nga bakolwe	backwards like monkeys.

My interpreter claims that entering backwards means that their job is not finished yet. Others say they represent monkeys, which enter sneaky, because they do not want to be seen, because it has to be secret what happened in the bush.

Here the seclusion from the village ends.

All women are standing with their backs against the wall. They are dancing and acting like they want to sit down. The girl is standing in the middle of the room. The women dance and sing that a girl is not allowed to sit down wherever and whenever she likes, but she has to wait until someone offers her a place to sit down. The *banacimbusa* is showing and pushing the girl how to stand and how to sit. After this all the women sit down. They get *kangala*, the traditional beer.

The *banacimbusa* and the sister of the girl's mother, who is the classificatory mother (my interpreter), start dancing in the middle of the room. They sing that her mother is happy because her daughter is back.

Yande yande yande twababantutu	It is great, it is great
yande mayo, yande twababili	It is great mother, now we are two
yande mwana mayo ine	Great mother, now we are three
yande mayo twabababili	

My informants say this song means that the girl is mature now and belongs to the world of women. It also means that she is capable of bearing children. I think it also refers to the matrilineal system. It can also mean that she will be married soon. The next song also refers to the strong bond between mother and daughter.

Pamwana webeli ndeya	Whatever may come, I will be there for my
mukutoloka nangu ndwele	(first born) daughter to celebrate.

Two women take a pestle and mortar and act like they are pounding food, while dancing on their knees. After this, the girl has to do this together with the *banacimbusa*.

Mukolwe tanina mayo ee naleloline,	A man cannot sleep with his mother, the
lelo anina kumukolobondo	rooster has found someone irresistible to
	satisfy his desires.

My interpreter says that it means that the husband is not supposed to have a girlfriend. The pestle and mortar are symbols of the ideal couple, united in body and soul.

One of the women is chewing tobacco and asks others to fetch more tobacco for her. They refuse and there is a quarrel again. They sing that a girl should never ask for anything, and never be irresponsible or have bad habits like smoking or chewing tobacco.

The *banacimbusa* brings in the pumpkin seeds, groundnuts, maize and the medicine and puts it on a fire. All the women sit on their knees, with their hands open in front of them. They are thanking for the medicine and the seeds.

Two women are putting one of each type of seed in the girl's mouth. While feeding her, they give her the instruction that when she is having her monthly period, she is not allowed to add salt, because otherwise the ones who eat the food she has cooked, will get ill.

Two women undress the girl, so that only her abdomen is covered. The *banacimbusa* rubs the girl with the medicine - the bark of the *mubwilili* tree, which is pounded and warmed on a fire - saying that this will protect her from swelling.

The *banacimbusa* says that it protects the girl from illness of the belly, because the medicine from this tree (*mubwilili*), is known to cure "stomach ache", which also means ache of the womb. It probably stimulates the menstrual cycle, because they said "when the period comes again next month, the medicine has worked." The medicine can also mean that the spirit of the menstrual blood is chased away, so she is clean now. However, the spirit should not be chased away too far, because it has to come back. Thus there is an ambivalence between the good and evil of the menses. It is polluting but also denotes to fertility and the creative power of women.

This ambivalence can also be seen in the seclusion of the girl: she has to be separated from the community, because she can harm others, but there is also a celebration and happiness about her menstruation.

While the woman is rubbing the girl, she gives her instructions. From now on she is not allowed to eat together with children, and she always has to sit with her back against something, like a wall or a tree, but never in the middle of a room, because otherwise children can walk behind her back, which can cause infertility. After she has been anointed with the medicine, she is allowed to eat, but not food that contains blood, like meat.

I think that things associated with blood, fire and sex are particularly dangerous for her because she is supposed to have her first menstruation and she is in liminality.

The food is brought into the room, Most of the women are drunk. It is dark in the room, lit only by a small candle. The women are dancing around the food and singing

Tabalya ngabwali kubala	Do not just eat without saying thanks
mwatotela mulompwe	

My interpreter tells me that "one should be patient, when food is brought in one is supposed to wait until one is asked to eat." Two women are dancing and with their mouths they take the lids of the plates. They go on with dancing and quarrelling, while the girl is sitting in the corner of the room. It takes a long time before they start eating. The food is *nshima* (pounded maize), beans and chicken. While they are eating, they sing a song saying that "beans are the best relish, there can never be a ceremony or a party without beans, even if there are many guests, beans will always be enough, beans should always be served."

The *banacimbusa* gives some food to the girl, who can eat by herself and has to stay in the corner while the others are eating.

Although the girl is not covered, she is still secluded, sitting in the corner. After the meal they sit, drink and quarrel. At 10 p.m. they go home.

The second day of the initiation rite

On the second day, the women are making the clay models and drawings (*mbusa*) in the grandmother's house. There is no ritual for the girl. She is allowed to walk near the house and is only allowed to speak when she is asked something. She is not allowed to speak about the initiation rite.

The grandmother of the girl is making clay. Three women are making red, black and white paint. After a meal and a lot of talking they start their job.

First the *banacimbusa* puts some white paint on the foreheads of all the women and on me, because "we are in the *chisungu* (initiation) now." She tells me that white is the colour of purity.

Then the *banacimbusa* and an assistant start making drawings on a wall, with the paint they just made, while the others make clay models. They put beans in the clay models. At last they put white powder over all the models. In the meantime they are singing and drumming. Some of them put up their *citenge*, and show and touch their backsides while dancing.

According to the women the beans are just to make it look nice, but I think they use beans because of their symbolic meaning (see page 48). They said that the colours red, black and white in the drawing did not have a special meaning. However, Turner (1976), Richards (1956) and Corbeil (1982) noticed that red symbolises among others menstrual blood and hunting, black represents death and white means purity, fertility, without bad luck. The Nazarethi used to wear a white uniform. (Uniforms were abolished by the bishop in 1989). Now only the white head-dress is allowed. I think the white uniform also symbolises purity and fertility and is associated with initiation rites.

The women are discussing and talking a lot about how to draw and how to make the models. It looks as if they did not really know how to do it, except for the *banacimbusa* and one assistant. I noticed the same the day before in the bush. The next day it was different.

The third day of the initiation rite

The third day is also the last day of the initiation rite. During daytime, the *banacimbusa* and the three assistants finish the drawings. The girl stays in another room. In the evening the ritual starts again, and it goes on during the night till the next morning.

During the ritual, the parish priest, who was eager to see the rite, was allowed to witness a small part of it. This was only after a long discussion. The women said they could not refuse such an authority. Therefore they allowed him to act like the future husband of the girl. It is exceptional that they let the priest in.

During the ritual the women explained the drawings, clay models and the acts to me. My interpreter told me some of the meanings, but because she did not know them all, the *banacimbusa*, who spoke English, explained most of the subjects. Sometimes, other people also said some of the meanings, e.g. when the *banacimbusa* was busy with the performing of an act in the rite, which was then explained to me through my interpreter. I will describe their explanation chronologically, which implies that the drawings, clay models and acts are described alternately.

> The women enter the room where the initiation rite will be performed, and now they cover the big circular *mbusa* (clay model, see Picture 4) with a *citenge* and the drawings with a mat.
> The women start dancing, talking and drinking beer. Three women are leaving the room to fetch the girl. The women start arguing, saying that some of them are not good *banacimbusa*. They start drumming and singing
>
> | | |
> |---|---|
> | *Awee ngana pita* | I passed the border of the Bemba |
> | *napita mulu bemba mulyamwine* | and I heard noises from the drums |
> | *naufwa bele bele ee* | "Come, hear the drums, |
> | *naufwa bele bele muli ngoma* | it is good to learn." |

Here they refer to the Bemba tradition and claim that the initiation is a Bemba rite. Particularly in town this is irrelevant, but it also shows that ethnicity is important.

The women who went to fetch the girl stay away a long time. Later on they explained that they were discussing with the parish priest, who wanted to enter the house. He was eager to see the initiation rite. He wanted to go in right away, but he was only allowed later on and only for one act.

> Three hours after the women came, the girl is brought in. She is on her knees behind the *banacimbusa*, covered with a blanket. While she is brought in, the women sing:
>
> | | |
> |---|---|
> | *Ine ndi kabwa nsende fipe* | "I am a snail, I take many things on me |
> | *ntwale ku bakulu* | we have brought you a silver bath." |

> The *banacimbusa* and the girl are sitting on their knees under the blanket, then they leave the room. They come in again in the same way, and now the *banacimbusa* brings in a plate with beans. They put their heads on the floor, left-right-left. The girl is put in a corner, still covered.
> They sing a song, saying that everyone should give some money before they can start. The *banacimbusa* goes around dancing with a plate, so everyone can put some money on the plate. The women are drumming and ululating.

Then the *banacimbusa* takes off the blanket of the girl. She is rubbed in with white powder and is wearing a *citenge* around her abdomen. My informants say that in the past the girl was painted, but now they only put white powder on her.

They do the "fishing", like they did on the first day.

The *banacimbusa* is pulling the ears of the girl, saying that she must listen and use her ears. They sing:

Nalelo tubanbe ngoma	Again, today let us rejoice ourselves
chilichisu ma twangale mwansabansa	again, today let us play the drums
nalelo tumubambe ngoma	

My informants say it means: another one has her first period, so we have to do our job, let us do it with joy. Another meaning is: If you do not listen, we will beat you like a drum.

The girl is put back in the corner, covered with a blanket and behind the mat covering the drawings.

After they have put out the candles, so that it is dark in the room, the fictive future husband, in this case the parish priest, is allowed to enter the room, while the women sing

Kalombo wemushonko wile kuteba	Kalombo, you servant,
taulabwela	why haven't you returned
kalombo wemusha wile kuteba	from where you went to fetch firewood
taulabwela	

My informants explain that this song represents the entering of the husband to be for the first time in the house of the initiation. Another meaning is that a husband must expect to do some of the woman's work especially when she is pregnant. When she needs something or she does something wrong he must be kind. After she has given birth his duties of doing the woman's work will end.

They put on a light and then they sing

Peniko akamwenge kabweshe	Give me a light even if it is small
nangu kali kace sanikile mayo	it will allow me to see my mother

My informants say that this song refers to the first sight of the future wife.

I think "mother" refers to the mother of his future children, or to the fact that she has to look after him as a mother. To call someone "mother" is also a sign of respect.

Three women start dancing around the big circular *mbusa*, and with their mouths they take off the *citenge*.

Awe nachisungu ba lamuntanshya uku	Nachisungu they honour your beauty
wama	but I have not seen you.
shamumwene	Give me a light so I can see you.
peni umwenge sanikile mayo wandi	
shamumwene	

My informant says that the song means that for the first time the girl is going to see the clay models and the beauty of the paintings. *Nachisungu* refers both to the girl and to the

60

mbusa. I think it also means that it is the first time the girl will be uncovered, so she can be seen.

Before the women want to start, they have to pay. Some of the women put money around the big *mbusa*. Two women are dancing, while they take away the mat which covered the drawings (Picture 1). Then they put their faces on the floor, left-right-left.

Mulangile mulange amone	Show her everything about the *mbusa*
inganda yambusa, mulanga amone	let us teach her everything we know
amona yambusa, mulange amone	

Two women are walking in the wedges of the circular *mbusa*. Then the girl has to do this, while the *banacimbusa* and an assistant take the girl by the hand while they are walking in the *mbusa*.

Nayenda eenda mutu koko inee	I have walked so much,
molu yakalipa	my legs are painful
mayo ule eenda shani ifiwa eenda ee	my feet are hard
mulo yakapila	

The big circular *mbusa* represents the marriage and the house. My interpreter says that its wedges are the steps in the life of a married woman, the steps she has to take, and the difficulties she will experience in life, everything she has to go through. The parts are small, which means that she has to take small steps, and that she has not enough space to walk, meaning that she will experience many problems. She is not supposed to run away for problems, but she has to go on with her marriage until she dies. The phallus symbol in the middle is the symbol of the husband, the feather on top of it represents the beauty of the woman.

It may also mean that the woman is the pivot on which the household hinges.

Men are identified as hunters, symbolised in ritual as lions. For instance when the women went into the bush and saw the special tree they were looking for, they acted as if they were hunting, and in the house they sang songs about a lion.

With a bow and arrow the priest has to "pierce" a drawing which at one level represents the eyes of the girl. The future husband has to shoot to proof his fertility.
At another level this drawing represents the womb.
The red circles denote that it is taboo to have sexual

Drawing 1. **The eyes**

intercourse while blood is shed during menstrual periods or after childbirth, the white spot in the middle denotes the fertile and right times to have sexual intercourse. This symbol is called "the bull's eyes", because it is very difficult to shoot in the eyes of a bull.

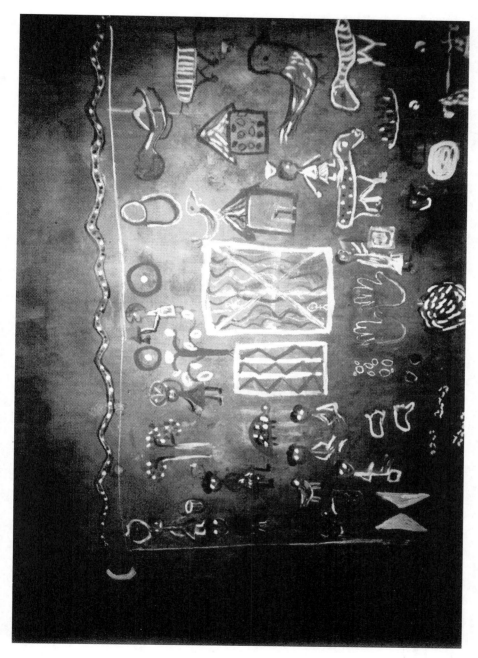

Picture 1. *The drawings on the wall*

The various components will be discussed specifically below

Picture 2. *Clay models (1)*

Picture 3. Clay models (2)

63

Picture 4. *Circular mbusa*

Picture 5. *Assistant showing the drawings*

Picture 6. *The girl is taking the seeds from the soil*

Picture 7. *The girl is rubbed with white powder*

> *Tata koni tata koni*
> *kali kwi kalafye kali kwi kalafye*
> *mayo koni mayo koni*

> The bird was just sitting nicely
> on its place.

My informants say that it means that the girl has to say good-bye to her virginity and has to be purified. "The bird was just sitting", means that she was a virgin. A bird often refers to the girl.

> *Ka ndoshe nama yandi*
> *taibula mwine walasa*

> Let me smell my meat
> there is no animal shot without an owner.

My informants say that the meaning is that the husband can take her, she belongs to him, he is responsible for her. The girl has to wait for the hunter, her future husband.

Actually this is a part of the wedding ceremony (see chapter three). It is very unusual that the parish priest acted as the future husband. After this he had to leave, because men and unmarried people are not allowed. He refuses to leave. There is a long discussion. It ends up that he has to pay a large amount of money and the girl has to leave the room while she is still covered. She is not allowed to be in the room with a man. The women start to discuss how they are going to explain the *mbusa*. They just sing the songs, but there seems to be no sequence in it. Sometimes the women stop and argue with the priest that he has to leave. The priest refuses and after having paid more money he gets more symbols explained. All the drawings on the wall, except the snake and the moon, are in a white square, which means that all the drawings inside concern things in or around the house.

The drawing of a woman with a basket on her head and a basket in her hand means that she should not leave her husband when there are problems. A clever woman is always near her husband. Show respect to the husband. The basket on her head represents the marriage, which she should honour, and also the in-laws, which she should treat with respect, The basket in her hand represents her own relatives, which she should not forget.

If she treats one kingroup better than the other, the other will leave her, so she will be dependent on only one group, which is not good. The husband comes first, the parents and relatives are second. A woman needs her brain to keep the marriage, otherwise the marriage will fail. The pad on top of the head represents the brain.

Drawing 2.
Woman with basket on head and basket in hand

> *Chilya chaya*
> *chasha catuka abalume*
> *chilya chaya*
> *akachenjele kalimwisamba*
> *lya balume kaletenya*

> There she goes,
> after insulting her husband,
> a clever one is with her husband
> enjoying him.

> *Chupo walemene ngana*
> *umukowa eeoo wasenda*

> In marriage you carry the pad on your head
> the relatives in your hands

The *banacimbusa* says that the drawing of the fingermillet is a sign of love. It is drawn as two different parts, which means a man and a woman having different tasks which should not be crossed, but are supposed to be harmonious and well- balanced. Love is good, but the wife should make love only with the husband. Millet is an important cereal.

Drawing 3.
Fingermillet

In my opinion the branches also symbolise the genitals of man (left) and woman (right).

Drawing 4. **The snake**

The *banacimbusa* says that the snake represents the man. He is the one the girl will be married to, so she has to stay with him. She is not supposed to jump over him, meaning she is not supposed to pass the boundary of marriage. She has to stay of marriage with one man only. The small and big spots in the snake represent the small and big problems she will face in her marriage. The white spots refer to the good things in marriage, the black spots refer to the problems in marriage, the red ones to the dangerous and menstrual periods. The waves of the snake represent the ups and downs in a marriage. It is drawn on top of the white square (the house), meaning that the husband is the head of the house. It is a sign of commitment and relationship. The snake is also a sign of danger and sexuality, he comes to seduce.

The moon, which is drawn outside the white square, represents the woman. She is the light. It also represents the menstruation and means that the menstruation should not be seen. If the girl is married, she is allowed to have sex in the house whenever she wants. She is not supposed to go out in the evening until she is married. An unmarried girl is not supposed to have sex. The moon is drawn next to the snake, as though the snake (man) is attracting the moon (woman).

Drawing 5.
The moon

The drawing of the eagle (some say a leopard) symbolises the penis which should be strong and erect. The eagle represents strength. A woman is supposed to love her husband for the way he makes love to her. His penis gets strong just like the eagle when it is catching its pray.

Drawing 6.
The eagle

Turner (1967, 73) notes that black is associated with sexuality. I think it also means that when the husband is old, he can still have sex and is still fertile.

Mwatemenwa kufita nelyo kulile	The eagle I like it for its blackness
mwakole mwatemenwa ukufita	although it is old
nangu kotele mwatemenwa ukufita	

The drawing of the tortoise (*fulwe*) means that one should be generous. If a friend has a problem, one should put out the neck, when you have problems, keep the head inside. Do not meddle with other people's business. Do not look in the pots what people are eating, but give food when someone is visiting you. Be hospitable. So it is a symbol of generosity, reticence, prudence and humility. One should act like a team in marriage; do not exclude the kingroup or the in-laws.

Drawing 7.
The tortoise

Fulwe pa fyakwe, aingisha mukoshi mu cifwambako	The tortoise for its own things gets its head into its shell
pa fya banakwe	but for its friends "things"
akolomona umukoshi mu cifwambako	it puts its neck out off its shell.

The drawing of the dog means that a woman should not talk too long with a friend, because otherwise the dog will eat the food. Do not start talking before the food is ready, because the food will be burned or the pot can break. Others say she should not go barking like a dog, or gossiping while she has not taken care of her family. When she has problems with her husband, she is not supposed to run away or tell others, because it will bring more trouble.

Drawing 8. **The dog**

There is a play act, in which a woman, dressed up as a man, with an overall, boots and a helmet, comes in. She creeps on the floor and stumbles, like she/he is drunk. She/he asks for food. A woman gives it, (handing over two plates, cups and spoons). The 'man' starts complaining: "Is this all I get? I have given you money." The woman says that the dog has eaten it, because she has stayed away too long. The man says: "You stupid wife."

Mayo nachikalishya	the lazy woman,
walekele mbwa yalya munani	see the dog has eaten our food

The drawing of two women shows that women are supposed to have long genitals. They are proud of them. It shows that the female genitals are important. It also means that when a girl has her menarche, she is supposed to (go to the bush and) tell someone, a woman she can trust, but not her mother nor a close relative. This means that she is not supposed to talk about sexual things with her mother. Another woman says that it means that it is bad to have a secret love, it can bring people fighting and ends in death.

Drawing 9.
Two women

Mwana ngakula talanga njina	Mother look,
mayo mona ifyonakula	I am mature now

Nachisungu pamo twakumanina	Nachisungu
chimba namucheche	here we have met in the swamp
muchelungu pamo twakumanina	do not go and tell anybody
ngolichitongo ukaye shimika	

The drawing of a man who is sewing his trousers symbolises that men can not look after themselves, so the woman should keep her husband tidy and look after his clothes because through him people will know his wife. My interpreter says that If you do not keep your husband well, he will dress himself badly, his clothes will be dirty and worn out, and he will not be punctual any more. The *banacimbusa* says that the other meaning is that men do not learn anything. They dress themselves badly, meaning that men are irresponsible, and have to be looked after because they cannot look after themselves. They are "foolish". The song refers to a man who does not like to see the problems but only wants to drink. The wife tries to advise him but he will not listen.

Drawing 10.
Man sewing trousers

> *mwaume ushifwa milandu*
> *chaikalila ukubila*

> The man who does not listen,
> he only likes drinking

My interpreter says that the drawing of the woman with a basket on her head means it is not easy to start to live with a man. You must always have something to lean on, because the marriage is a heavy load. The ideas you get about it, are given by the culture.

Drawing 11.
Woman with basket on head

> *Monachisungule ee chifina*
> *nalya chisungule ee chafina*

> The problems are
> too heavy for me

My interpreter says that the drawing of the bird (*kabangula*) on the roof of the house means that the bird watches the woman, symbolising the *banacimbusa* watching the girl. She should honour the *banacimbusa*, keep the rules and stick to one partner. The *banacimbusa* says that the bird refers to the girl, who should keep the problems inside the house. The house means that a woman has her own house, she should not tell others what happens in her house and not interfere with others. Another woman says that the meaning is that the house looks beautiful on the outside, but inside it has many problems. So do not admire things which you can not have, be happy with what you have.

Drawing 12.
The bird on the roof

> *Koni pamutenge kalya*
> *kashyakwe mbusa kalya*

> The bird on top of the roof

> *Ifya mu butala ulefimona*
> *ifya mu mutima tawafimone*
> *wailongela ilonge*

> What is outside you will see
> What is in my heart you will not see.

The drawing of the house is about the same as the other house: the woman is not supposed to tell others how she and her husband are living and what they are doing. The house has a roof, which means the inside should be covered or secret; it should be like the heart, and the mouth should not say what the heart knows. Everything in the house is for the husband, meaning that she is not supposed to tell others how the husband behaves, e.g. if he is drunk or does not have enough money. They emphasised that this is very important.

Drawing 13.
The house

Nama tenya, nama tenya
munganda ushilalaee waikalila namatenya
leka kutenya, namatenya

Stop interfering in other peoples problems.

Strong mystic links exist between husband and wife (Richards 1956, 34). Men and women are thought to be mutually attractive and interdependent. The polarity of male and female represents opposed qualities with direct relevance to the organisation of society.

The drawing of a woman who is delivering means that when a wife is pregnant the husband is not supposed to take a lover, because otherwise his wife will die from *ncila* (adultery). It is thought that when she has committed adultery she will die before delivery. When she dies in labour or just after she has given birth, her husband has committed adultery.

Drawing 14. **Delivering woman**

When a woman is pregnant it can be difficult for the husband, but still he should try to be understanding and not look for another girl.

Chile chile wandi
chile chile afwashani
chile chile afwa

Adultery,
my wife how did she die

The *banacimbusa* says that the drawing of a man and a woman with a stick between them means they are equal. The stick represents the balance between husband and wife. It means that in marriage one has to respect the own kingroup and the relatives of the husband. There has to be a balance between these two. Others said "women are like salt. One cannot eat relish without salt." Thus women are like salt,

Drawing 15.
Man and woman with stick

which means precious. Some say the woman points at the moon, meaning that when she follows the rules, her marriage will be like a new moon. In the drawing the husband walks ahead, the woman follows him.

The *banacimbusa* tells me that the big bird represents a bird called *mungumba* or *ichipululu*. This bird sings early in the morning, so it means that this is the best time to have sexual intercourse. At this time she can wake up her husband and ask him to have sex, because she is his wife.

Drawing 16. **Big bird**

Shimungumba ee wikele mona	Man look where you are sitting,
shimungumba shishi muna ilomo	man shake the dust

The *banacimbusa* says that the drawing of the black bird with a white ring around its neck is a sign of love. It means that when a woman is young and beautiful, it is easy to love her. When she gets old the husband should still love her, although she is ugly. It does not matter what you look like; what counts is the way you look after your husband. Men like women to have good manners. The beauty is inside. It also means that she should respect old people and she must not forget that one day she will also be old.

Drawing 17. **Black bird**

We chimwana chakubipa techotakila	You say I am ugly
abanobe	to your friends
shibwalya makasa yangombe	but you show off
meno yakubipa eyoo takila banobe	
shibwalya makanda ee	

The difference and the relations between the generations of women are shown. The girl is given the spirit of maturity, symbolised by the passing of a bridge, e.g. the clay-model of the bridge.

Initiation rites are concerned with adult sexuality and marriage, which are related to fertility. Sexuality is based on harmony between husband and wife. Many symbols refer to sexuality. In the drawings two symbols referring to fertility are central surrounded by other symbols of which some refer to sexuality.

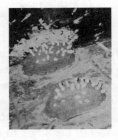

Model 1. **The bridge**

The *banacimbusa* says that the drawing of the *mupundu* tree, which is a tree which bears many fruits, is a sign of fertility. (It is the same tree as in the bush.) It is both female and male, meaning that men and women are equal. One should act like a team in marriage and not exclude the kingroup or the in-laws. It is a sign of love, and also means that a couple should vary the moments and ways of sexual

Drawing 18. **The mupundu tree**

intercourse.

The *banacimbusa* explains to me that the big rectangle in the centre of the drawings represents the bed. The song says that when a husband sleeps with another woman, you can not do anything (not have intercourse), he will leave you. Thus a woman should take care of her husband, so that he will stay with her and the couple can make love.

Drawing 19. **Big rectangle**

Nde yooha isalu yandi	I will burn my *citenge*,
akasuba mwatana impombo	you refused me bush meat

It means that a woman has no excuse to refuse her husband, so do not say that you do not feel well. If you do not want to have sex, you had better go back to your parents.

The small rectangle next to it represents the floor, meaning that a couple can make love everywhere in their house.

Both rectangles have white and red zig-zag lines, representing fertile periods and the periods when it is taboo to have intercourse. Other women say the zig-zag figures represent the labia. (This is only explained in the wedding ceremony.)

Drawing 20.
Small rectangle

The drawing of two animals resembling each other means that husband and wife are equal, only their shape is different. The genitals are drawn different, meaning that men and women are made to have intercourse and are one in sexual intercourse.

Drawing 21. **Two animals**

Others say "The animals are eating from one plate, which means that a husband should eat what his wife cooks for him." The *banacimbusa* says there is also a sexual meaning; the plate represents the womb, meaning that a couple should share only one womb.

So it means that the husband must be faithful to his wife.

The drawing of the "plate", which others say it is a field, means that one can solve a problem, but tomorrow there will be another one. Education goes on, the job of the *banacimbusa* will never end.

Drawing 22.
The field

Mwana wandi libala	My child is like a field,
umwana ee	I turn the grass grow
nati tabataba lyamena	

The drawing of the zebra (some say hyena) has also two meanings. The first is that a woman is not supposed to be idle, because being so people will say that she is bad, not beautiful, she will not marry and people will laugh at her, and she will become ugly. She is supposed to know her duties and responsibilities as a wife and future mother. Another meaning is opposite: the girl should be proud, she is beautiful like her parents.

Drawing 23.
The zebra or hyena

Others say that a zebra represents different colours and is a sign of beauty. A girl is beautiful when she is young. When a husband takes another lover, his wife can tell him that she was as beautiful as her when she was young, so what he sees in his girlfriend, he used to see in his wife. Her husband should not leave her for she is still the same woman. It also means that she should respect old people and she should not forget that one day she will also be old.

Yangu munkoloto	You servant zebra, showing your mane
kunto mwansa ee, kunto mwansa ee	
wamushya munkoloto, kunto mwansa ee	

Chisongo nangu mbalale ee	Zebra I may have changed my colours
umutoto umo	but my umbilical cord is still the same
chisongo nangu mbalale ee	

It is thought that the blood shed at menstruation and during childbirth has powerful qualities, but it is also polluting. Therefore it is taboo to make love while menstruating. Various symbols show this.

The drawing of a woman with a big red vulva is a warning that a woman should keep her vagina tight and dry. Her vagina should be pink. A red vagina is not good. If a husband wants to insult his wife, he calls her a big or red vagina, or says her labiae are small. Especially after a woman has given birth it is not good for a husband to be critical when having sex. He should not complain about her big vagina, because it was he who made her pregnant.

Drawing 24.
Woman with red vulva

Nangu munje ati mwalepa kwenu	My husband is insulting me
niwe chebamo	that my home is too far
mulume aletuka ati walepa kwenu	it is him who looks in it
niwe chebamo	

A "red vagina" refers to the menstrual period. It is considered very bad to insult someone by referring to her period. It can be seen as a curse. Also women insult each other by saying that someone has a big vagina or small labiae. Women use herbs or a small piece of cloth to make the vagina dry. This was not explained to the girl, because the banacimbusa said that it was not good to use these things. It may also be left for the wedding ceremony. The home refers to the vagina.

The *banacimbusa* says that the drawing of the groundnuts means that the girl is an adult now. Although "women are small" like groundnuts, they have brains, they have wisdom and something to offer. This should not be hidden. The shell of the

Drawing 25. **Ground nuts**

groundnut can be thick, but the most important thing, the inner part, is good. Although the girl is still young, she has a lot of knowledge. Because she has learned, she is an adult now. Another woman says that the groundnut represents richness, it is valuable. Groundnuts are important for making food. The song means it does not matter if you have a small house that looks poor, what matters is that you and your husband have a good relationship, and you should keep it that way.

Tata ka lubalala ee
mwika mona uku tutumona ee
mu kati ee muli amano

Do not look at the shell of the groundnut
and think it has no value,
but look inside it.

The *banacimbusa* says that the drawing of the hands means that the hands are not only for the daily job, it is also nice to clean each other gently after having sex. The woman should clean her husband with her hands. She should put the sperm between her legs and clean his penis. (The latter is explained only in the wedding ceremony)

Drawing 26.
The hands

This shows that there is supposed to be intimacy during and after sexual intercourse.

Minwe yandi yaba nemilimo
minwe yandi akasuba yanya bwali
ubushiku yamansa amate
minwe yandi

These hands of mine work hard

The *banacimbusa* tells me that the drawing of the pot on the fire means that when the girl has learned but still does not know, she will not be a good woman. The song says that the meat in the pot will not be ready, there is still blood coming out of it. Like meat needs some time to be cooked, the girl who has just started to learn needs some time to learn all she has to know. Another meaning is that while having sexual intercourse it can happen that one of the partners does not have an orgasm, and one must accept this. While singing the song a woman takes two cups and a small piece of wood, representing a pestle and mortar, and starts pounding.

Drawing 27.
The pot on the fire

74

| Nangu mulimbike mukatondo | Do not hide your meat I do not eat it, |
| nama shikatato mulopa mukalongo | it smells of blood in the pot |

The women in the room claimed to have more knowledge than others which means having more authority. There was a competition among them. The *banacimbusa*s have to say who has conducted their own initiation rite, probably to show who was taught best. Then they yell and sing

| Nefye kumwensu chilawama | At our house we enjoy ourselves |
| fye balala mwikoma lyambusa | |

I think this song refers to the house of the initiation rite, where the *banacimbusas* enjoy themselves. It can mean that is good to be a *banacimbusa*, or be among women, or to have knowledge, but it may also refer to the fact that women are supposed to enjoy having a home and a family.

The drawing of a woman who is pounding means that when the husband is sleeping with another woman, the wife should not say anything about it. Even when someone comes to tell her, she should refuse to listen.

Drawing 28.
The pounding woman

Ulinanjina ee ulinanjina ee	The one with the mother
somone kabulangenti, chitensha	come and see
chitensha chitensha nangalimba	the man with the bedclothes
ulinanjina ee ulinanjina ee	he is moving

My interpreter says that the drawing of the feet (*mulangiliamoni*) means that a woman should not leave her husband, and the other meaning is that the girl should become like the women who teach her.

Someone else says the meaning is that it is good to have friends who care about you, otherwise you would walk into bad company.

awee ichi chipuba	This one is a fool,
tachi cheba kumakasa	she does not look where she goes
icha luba isoso	

Drawing 29.
The feet

The *banacimbusa* says that the clay model of a woman whose teeth stick out is called the jealous woman. Jealousy is not good, in marriage you need to trust each other and ignore small mistakes. Jealousy leads to divorce, so this is a warning not to be jealous. Another reason for her protruding teeth is that she talks too much. One is not supposed to talk about marital affairs with outsiders. A woman takes this *mbusa* in her hands and it is shown to all the women. Big teeth represent jealousy.

Model 2. **Woman**

| Nakailila ukufuba bwachitefi | Jealousy has done this to me |
| ngabwangalima kubufuba bwachitefi | |

My interpreter says that the clay-model of the lion (*mundu*) is also called the whistle. Two women dance while they hold the *mbusa* in their hands. They put it in the centre of the room and on their knees they dance towards it. It has a hole on both sides, and the two women blow in it. It is like a drum which spreads noise, meaning that whenever the girl hears rumours she should not believe or spread them. Particularly when someone tells her that her husband is having another wife, she should not allow them to say this, because he is her husband, so she should not believe

Model 3. **The lion**

bad things about him. Another woman says that the blowing in the clay model means that husband and wife have become one. This is also done in the wedding ceremony. The *banacimbusa* says that the lion is calling, because it wants to eat someone. Husband and wife can make love at any time. The woman must receive her husband. When a man wants to make love, he is like a lion: he is hungry.

Yalila kumusokoto   Cry from inside

The drawing of a rectangle with two white and two black triangles (chequered square) represents the two phases in a woman's life. It is a symbol of the girl leaving her parents to live with a man. She should solve her own problems. She can not go back.

I think that the black triangles represent the phase when she lived with her parents, who were responsible for her. The white triangles represent the phase when she stays with her husband, who will take care of her in the future. They also refer to the fertile periods of the adult and the good things in life.

Drawing 30.
Rectangle and triangles

Chipata ee chatupatula   The arse has separated

The drawing of a naked man and woman means that children should never enter the bedroom of their parents, because they are not allowed to see their parents naked. So before entering the bedroom they have to knock and ask permission to enter.
Two women are dancing, while the others sing:
"Children are not taught here where life comes from. Oh, you touch my beads which mother gave me." (I do not know whether this refers to the taboo on incest.)

Drawing 31.
Naked man and woman

This means various things: the girl is not supposed to take something out of someone's bag or pot but is supposed to ask before she can take. When children see her taking something they can tell their father. In the end, the children will have no respect for her. My interpreter says it means that she should not eat earlier than her husband. According to the *banacimbusa* there is also a sexual meaning as food is associated with sexuality. She should not take someone's husband.

Another woman says that after the girl is initiated she is not allowed to enter her parents' bedroom. She may see something which is not good for her.

Baiba kafunda kamuti mayo *ewa kafwaile* *abana bakuno ulupapashya*	They have stolen my medicine, the one my mother gave to me
Talaisa uyu mulwani *umwana anjebelela wiso kumwishi*	He has come, my child told me at the door
Mwana wa mulume *taliwa ala ubwafya alabika*	The man does not sleep without eating do not hide something for him.

The *banacimbusa* says that the drawing of the pot symbolises the penis of a man which is supposed to be erected while having intercourse (This is explained only in the wedding ceremony.)

Drawing 32. **The pot**

I think this also refers to the marital pot which is used for ritual cleaning, although this was not explained during the rite.

My interpreter says that the drawing of the figure of a woman and a man with an axe beside the tree has various meanings; one is that when the husband has another woman, his wife will say that she will kill herself with an axe. Another meaning is that the husband wants to divorce his wife, they can not get along. The *banacimbusa* says the meaning is that when the husband wants to meet his wife while she is having her menstrual period, she can say that he

Drawing 33. **Man, woman and axe**

should give her an axe so that she can take out her womb. It is considered very bad to have sex while the woman is having her period: it brings diseases, loosing weight, causing a child to die or bad cough.

Chimbale aleti tukanine *muka kaeela* *ee ebele uyu muka kaeela*	*Chimbale* let us go and have sex in the red sea
Leta kasembe komaule tata *mulume citemwe*	Bring the axe, I chop for my husband, he will be happy
Aka kumulomo *sotete chembe soteleee* *sotele chembe wekwashi yandi*	She likes too much gossiping, take her

Various symbols show that it is forbidden to commit adultery.

The *banacimbusa* says that the liver is a symbol of sexuality. The explanation was that sexuality is something between two people, a married couple. I think this is because the liver has two lobes, and also because this is inner-meat, which contains a lot of blood.

Drawing 34. **The liver**

The liver is the best part of meat, which is only given to the husband and (male) guests.

Mayo ilibu lya ngombe	This liver from the cow
lyakulya naba shimutale	is only for me and my husband

The *banacimbusa* says that the drawing of the razor and soap means that the wife and husband have to shave each others armpit hair and pubic hair. This has to be done by using hot water, a burning stick, razor or pair of tweezers. After this the wife has to anoint the penis with vaseline, and the couple is supposed to make love then. (This is only explained in the wedding ceremony)

Drawing 35. **Razor and soap**

Yansa kasengele tulale	Make the mat (bed) we sleep
abalume bele mukubamba	
yansa kasengele banee	

There is a break, and the priest has to leave the room. The girl is brought in, covered under a blanket behind the *banacimbusa*.

The song the women sing is about the snake who comes to seduce her. Some women are dancing with their hands behind their feet on the ground and their *citenge* high. They open and close their legs. The meaning is that the girl is supposed to keep her virginity, until someone has paid the bride price.

The women never showed their genitals, but always covered them with a *citenge* between their legs.

Sotambe chibale	Come and look at
ichiselela mumolu	the things that hang between the legs
sotamba chibale	

The meaning of this song is that it is very bad for children to see the parents' sex organs or parents having sexual intercourse.

Mayo kabambe	Mother I have eaten something
kababa munda	and it is aching in my stomach
mayo kabambe kashi kalabaee	
kababa munda	

The song means that it is easy to get pregnant now she is mature, but she is not supposed to get pregnant without being married.

It also means that if the husband gives her a disease, she should not hide this but tell others. This means that she is also to be respected: the husband cannot treat her as he likes.

Girls' initiation rites often have aspects of sexual license, privileged obscenity or mockery of men (La Fontaine 1986, 164). This is revealed through various symbols of the genitals of men and play-acts in which sexuality is made physically explicit. The women seemed to amuse themselves with it. This was only done after the priest had left.

The licentious behaviour of women is part of a sequence of actions which are not only manifestations of lack of respect for men, but also the reversal of normal feminine behaviour. Women are bound to be submissive and humble, but in the initiation rite they are allowed to be quite outrageous and to shout obscenities. These reversals are a part of initiation rites, marking the marginal period between the two states of being. This reversal is not a manifestation of feminine resentment against men, but must be seen as an opposition of symbols, a reordering of categories (cf. La Fontaine 1986). There is no hostility towards men in the *chisungu* (Richards 1956, 159). In considering the initiation rites of girls it is necessary to elucidate the components of a symbolic field that includes the idea of "women". Implicit in those meanings is a contrast with the cluster of ideas of "men". The women who are the performers of the ritual represent the whole range of associations, not merely the categories male and female (cf. La Fontaine 1986). This may be a reason why girls are only initiated by women.

The girl is "made a woman", which means that it is made clear to her that there is an element of equality between the initiate and the women, which is that they have the same body and genitals. This can be seen as the construction of womanhood.

Ibibili ibibili ibibili	I have grown now, I take light and give it
nakula nabulako ubunto ibibili	to the drummer.
napela wangoma ibibili chinpele wangoma	

This is a song in Lala, which show that there are also elements in the rite which are not Bemba, due to the mixing of people in the township.

Another woman sits in front of the girl, with her legs open and her *citenge* high, while she is pulling her *citenge*, like she is pulling her labiae and shows the girl how to do it. Then they turn round and show this to all the women, while the song is sung again. The girl is put against the wall.
The next song says: "I have two labia, I have worked on them, I was born with them, so I have prolonged them."

The extending of the labiae is often shown in this rite, which denotes that the labiae, the genitals of a woman, are important. They are so important that they are even made longer to accentuate them. Women are proud of them. They refer to sexuality, which means that they are supposed to enjoy sexuality and enjoy their body. It also refers to fertility. It may also refer to the matrilineal system, in which women are important.

The clay-model of a man with an erect penis shows the girl the male genitals, which she is only supposed to see when she is married. She should not be frightened when she sees a penis for the first time.

Two women dance with their *citenge* high up between their legs, one looks between her legs, the other one let others look between her legs. The song says that it is natural to have sex, so do not think that it is an illness. But if you have sex with many men, you will get a disease.

A woman is moving on all fours towards her. Her hands are moving like she is pounding grain with her

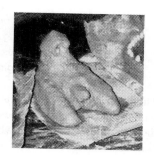

Model 4. **Man**

hands. She shows the girl how to do it by telling her and moving her. Later on that night two women and the girl are doing this again while turning around in a circle. My interpreter says that there are many boys who are like flies and come to see the girl who was hidden up till now. When a fly is disturbing her she should keep on pounding the millet.

The meaning is that when she is having her period, she is not clean. It is an incitement to hygiene.

Chisempele chaikala mulukolo mayo monako chakomanako chisempele chaikala munona chalobanako, mayo monako	The bird leaves the veranda, mother look, the bird stays in the river and disappears, mother look.

This song means that men know that she is mature, so they are following her. They just want to take advantage of her and want to make love, but she is not allowed to have a child without a father.

Mumbwe alila owee wasenda ipapa chilya teti basende iyi papa yali kumana matako	The hyena has stolen the *citenge* he should not have done this

This means: Take care of your period materials, its is not nice for others or even dangerous to see them. People told me that menstrual blood makes a woman particularly vulnerable to witchcraft.

Two women play that they are quarrelling. The song the others sing says that she should never insult her parents or older people, she is not supposed to stand in front of elder people, but she should kneel down, she should not sit just everywhere, she has to be humble and kind.

There is a play of a woman who sits on a chair. Another woman pushes her off the chair, and puts the girl on it. Then the girl is put against the wall again.

A woman tells the girl the meaning of this, which is that she may be proud of her property, but someone else can take it.

A woman enters the room on all fours, while another woman holds a pot on the back of the first woman. The song says: "Do not socialise with men, wait until your future husband comes to you. A woman says to the girl: "my vagina is for everyone. Whenever I see a man, I open my vagina."

The women "explain" the drawings to the girl while she sits with her back against the wall with the drawings, so she does not see them. This underlines that the rite is not so much for the girl, but for the women who perform it. By "explain" I mean: pointing at the drawings, singing the songs and performing acts.

Two women dance on all fours. One of them has a white bracelet in her mouth, and the other woman tries to take it out with her mouth. Then the girl is put on her knees in the centre of the room, and she has to move her hips. She has to take the bracelet out of the woman's mouth, while the *banacimbusa* holds the girl's hands on her back. The woman moves her head to make it difficult for the girl to take the bracelet. After a while she manages to take the bracelet, and then she has to do it again. Now she manages to take it faster. The *banacimbusa* puts the girl on the floor, left right left. Then she says "you woman" to the girl and puts her back against the wall.

This is the first time that she is called "woman", so she has grown now, but she is still in liminality.

The song says: "Oh big bird, come, I will be your wife." It means that wherever the husband goes, he will come back. When she is married, she must wait for her husband. She should not have a lover, not even when her husband is away from home for a long time, because he will return to her.

Mayo nakasasanya muchalo ukekalemo	My child, try to live in this difficult world
munganda yasolo kekalemo	

Another item is that she is supposed to keep a secret.

Twalanda bonse ngoli chitongo	We have talked in secret,
ukaye landa iwee	if you have no brains,
ukaye shimika iwee	you will tell others

The *banacimbusa* pulls the girl on her feet to the middle of the room and waves the girl's feet with her hands, pulls the girl's arms and waves the girl's feet again. Then she pulls the girl's ears and nose, and again the girl's feet with her own feet, like she is kicking the girl. Then the *banacimbusa* feels the girl's breasts. After this she puts the girl on the floor left right left.

The song says that she is not supposed to show of. "You are not beautiful, you generation of the cattle. You come from our generation, our ancestors, and there was nothing special about it. So whatever you are, you came from this generation." The *banacimbusa* whispers to the girl that she should keep this song in her mind.

Natonyako kumabele yababemba	I have touched the breasts of a Bemba
mukolwe pikioo	

My informants claimed that the pulling of the breasts, which was done several times by different women, was to check whether the girl had slept with a man; in that case the breasts would be weak. It was also said to be just teasing to make the girl humble. I think it also refers to the matrilineal system of the Bemba and the importance of her breasts now for nourishment by breast-feeding and, moreover, it is done to denote that she starts to be a woman and has a female body.

The *banacimbusa* and another woman play act with a flat round *mbusa*, where they have put in three pieces of clay and some beans. Both of them try to take the plate. One of them puts the clay under the plate, representing fire. The *banacimbusa* sits on the floor. Suddenly she runs around with the *mbusa*. Then she and two others are dancing with the *mbusa* in their hands.

This means that food can only be eaten after it is cooked. The food shrinks through cooking, it leaves the best parts, so one has to wait until the food is cooked. Food for your husband should be prepared carefully. When one has only little food, one should keep something for another time.

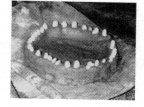

Model 5. **Plate**

The *mbusa* represents the food cooked for the husband, but also the womb. Food is associated with sexuality. Food may symbolise the girl, who is grown up now and is fertile.

The *banacimbusa* and another woman are dancing while they take the *mbusa* in their hands. It means that she must receive her husband, the wife cannot refuse her husband. After having sexual intercourse the woman should thank her husband. She is not allowed to say his name, but she should address to him saying *mukwai*. This word is a sign of respect and is generally used for every adult.

Nga mwashita ulupe bambi batila ayee mukwai	When you buy a bowl, some people do say thank you

A woman is play-acting, dancing wildly, miming, asking, suddenly stops, and starts dancing again. She holds her *citenge* high up between her legs and holds her legs open, right before the girl's face. The song says that when her husband is poor, there is no need to admire him. Before going elsewhere, take care of your vagina.

This means that when the husband does not satisfy her, she can have a lover. She has a right to be satisfied, and her husband should take care of her. This denotes the autonomy of women and contradicts subservience.

Butanda ndeka na kumbya nama kwisano	Mat let me go, I have admired fresh meat at the chiefs place

My informants told me that in the past, after having killed an animal, they first went to the chief to give him a part. I do not know whether this song refers to the past or is just a song because it is familiar to them.

After the items of sexuality and her body, which denotes that the construction of womanhood has almost finished, the girl is put back again, she is still in the liminal phase.

A play of a woman sitting on a *citenge* on the floor. She holds a mirror in her hand, stands up, dances, lays down again, acting as if she is idle.

Mwanawandi munangani nakatangala pabutanda nakatangala ee nakatangala pabutanda	My child is lazy, she just likes laying on the mat

The meaning is that a wife is supposed to work and cook for her husband, but she is just lazy.

One woman tickles the girl under her feet. Then she dances in front of her. Three woman are holding sticks in their hands while singing this. The girl is put in the middle of the room, by pulling her by her feet. The women are dancing around her, beating the sticks on the floor. If she has been a good girl, someone will pay for her so that she will not be beaten.
The classificatory mother is giving some money, but the women say that she has to wait, because she is too fast. The women go on beating on the floor, then they fall on the floor as a sign of respect.

Nabwikele tiyetumone ngabalikutenwa iwee nabwikele sasabuka iwee tiyetimone ngabalikutenwa iwee	The sitting girl who they are drumming for let us go to your home and let us see if they love you.

Here the women show their power. They can ask as much money as they like, or they can beat the girl as long as they want. It denotes that the girl is still not the same as they are. It is also a way to show that they want the girl to keep the moral things they teach. They are responsible for the girl.

The girl is put on her feet and has to stand with her arms open against the wall. A woman is dancing in front of the girl, while knocking on the girl's throat, saying: "say ah." This the girl does, together with the woman. The song goes: "Cry like a baby, so that your voice will be different from the way it was."

According to my interpreter she has to cry like a child, because they have told her many things, she has learned a lot, so she becomes another person now. She should not be shouting, but she must have a soft voice. The girl is put back against the wall by the *banacimbusa*.

Mwangalila leta umunganga njingilemo mwangalila	Mwangalila bring the woman I enter

Mwangalila is an animal that makes a specific sound after making love. The women could not explain this to me. According to the dictionary Chibemba-English (published by Ilondola Language Centre, 1993) *mwangalila* also means amusement, rejoicing. Thus I think the song refers to enjoying to make love.

Umunganga refers to a woman, but also means traditional healer and leader, so it can also refer to the *banacimbusa* or meaning that the girl can start being a *banacimbusa* herself. Here the girl becomes equal to the women.

A woman makes the girl stand up again. Two women are dancing around her, while they put stones in her mouth. When the song is finished they take the stones out of her mouth and the girl is put back on the floor. According to my interpreter it means that she should act as if she does not see what she is not supposed to see, she has to keep a secret.

Nalelo tumubambe ngoma	Very far it is the eyes of the bird
twa kumumona mwansabamba	which are looking not looking like fire

A woman sits in front of the girl and teaches the girl how to "dance". She puts a shawl around her hips, to accentuate this part of her body. She teaches her the "bed-dance", which is supposed to be danced to attract her husband. The dance is done on the knees as well as standing on the feet.
The song says that she is lucky, because she has been taught how to dance.
They put a *citenge* on the floor in the middle of the room. Two women act as they are making love. The girl is covered under the blanket, so she does not see the act.

Chimbaya mbaya chabuka,	The motor is awake,
sheshe umwana pakanti	let me move my child and we sleep
chimbay ambaya chabuka, sheshe	
umwana tulale	

The meaning is: I can feel the moving of my husband, so let me put the child aside and have sex. (Usually a mother lays in bed with her child.)

The miming of sexual acts in ritual context is to be understood as a means by which the ritual action is infused with potency and generative force. Sexual symbolism is not so much a reference to sexuality and fertility as an attempt to use immaterial powers for social purposes. In the initiation rite is it used to induce change. This explains why it is mimed in the initiation rite, although the girl is warned not to have sexual intercourse. The latter is also a Catholic value, while the miming of sexual acts contradicts Catholic morals. These acts are performed towards the end of the rite. The girl has "grown" and is to know the things about sexuality now.

Then they put the girl in the middle of the room, where she has to lay down. They put a *citenge*, branches and leaves on her, so that the girl is totally covered. They dance around her, while singing: "This woman was sleeping without dancing".

The *banacimbusa* explains that this means that when a man wants to marry, he has to go to his future in-laws. He can not find a girl in the street, because girls are not supposed to be in the streets. When she is married, she is supposed to be sexually active and do the "bed-dance", which is a special movement with her hips, to attract her husband before having intercourse.

Mubamba nalufya	My daughter is lost, who is going to help
naniwakunukwila ubowa	me
mubamba waluba	with picking mushrooms

It means that she is matured, so the mother is losing her now, because she will soon be married. The mother will be alone, she has no one to help her with her work.

This means that she will start a family of her own. It expresses a tension between mother and daughter in a matrilocal village of the past in which after some years the husband may decide to leave the village and take his wife with him. It refers to the neolocal marriage setting of today.

They take off the leaves and *citenge* and the girl's body is rubbed in with white powder. Then she is put against the wall.
After this, they sing a song that everyone is proud of this girl, all her relatives are happy because now she has knowledge.
They put the girl in the middle. A woman with her *citenge* high like shorts puts some of the clay of the *mbusa*, representing the river, in her "shorts". She is rocking this, saying: "Come and see what your father has in his trousers."

Model 6. **The river**

The meaning is opposite; she is not allowed to open her legs. Another meaning is that women have no male genitals, so women need men. Men and women are complementary.

However, the river also denotes that a girl should keep a distance from her father. There is a taboo on incest.

The river symbolises a boundary and also the cleansing of the girl that passes the boundary.

The *banacimbusa* takes the girl behind her back and they creep around the room. The women are singing that she should not forget what she has learned, if she wants to be a good woman. Then she is put back against the wall. Again the woman sing a song about the things women should learn, and again the girl has to creep behind the *banacimbusa*. Together they leave the room.
Then all the women start to dance.

Nde chitashani mukula sesee	Today it is so nice
lelo chamama	what I should say
Nde chitashani	

It means that the women are happy for the girl that she is mature now. There is an ambivalence with the previous act, where the mother's sad feelings were shown. It makes clear that maturity is both sad and happy, the child dies, the adult is born.

Outside a chicken is slaughtered by two women. The *banacimbusa* tells me that it can not be done by the girl, because it is a symbol of making love, which the girl only learns in the wedding ceremony.

Naleta mulondo mayo	I bring the fishermen mother
mukolwe nalishama	you can see me, the cock, I suffer
naleta mulondo tumumyone	
tata mutale nalichula	

The girl is brought into the room again.

Kwangala kwachi ulupwa	Relations with a good friend are even
ngechi chanda chawama	better than your own family

Now the girl is a member of the women's world, where there is solidarity among the women.

The girl has to learn to play the drums. After the short while they stop this.

Nachisungu waikala pangoma lelo ilishe   Girl, you sit on the drum today, beat it

The last part is the "coming out" of the girl, when her new status is recognised.

Then they are going to "show the girl" in the township. In the streets they dance and sing while they are walking. The girl is wearing a long *citenge* and a blouse now, because of the cold. They walk only a short time. It is 5.30 a.m. and there is hardly anyone in the street yet.

The meaning is that they want to show the girl to the community and tell everyone that she is grown up now. The fact that they showed the girl at a moment when everyone was still asleep, indicates that the meaning of the community is less important. Besides it is not clear to what community she should be shown. Also people did not really want many people to know, because then many of them would want to come and see the girl and celebrate the new membership.

When they come back to the house, the girl has to lay down, just before the entrance of the house, covered with a *citenge*. It is like she is dead, representing that the child is "dead" now. People have to give some money, symbolising the money that her future husband will pay for her, so that she becomes a real woman through marriage.

Tata wandi natashya	Father my father I call,
kuli tata wandi natashya	father help me, I am tired.

The father of the girl is important because he (and the mother's brother) have to give permission of the marriage of the girl. The grandmother, representing the girl's father who had died, gives some money to release the girl.

The *banacimbusa* shows her power. She can ask for more money or let the girl lay down for a long time.

For the first time reference is made to the father. It shows a contrast between the dominant men in a society where the line goes through the women and children belong to the mother's kingroup.

> One of the women put two *fitenge* tied together between herself and the girl, representing the umbilical cord. The woman holds one *citenge* around her waist, the girl holds the other one in her hands. They are running around together, outside the house. Her grandmother has to pay, then they stop running.

It represents the birth of the woman. This was not done by the *banacimbusa*, because otherwise the relation between the girl and the *banacimbusa*, being her second mother, would be too close.

> Inside the house, the girl is put against the wall again. A woman with a stone on her head asks the girl the names of her parents, the ones who have given birth to her. The girl says the traditional names of both her parents and has to repeat them. The girl has to stand, and the woman puts the stone on the girl's head. On her knees the girl has to go to all the women in the room, calling the names of her parents. Her grandmother, who is standing in the doorway takes the stone off her head. One of the women tells the girl that she always has to remember the names of her parents, because they are the ones who have reared her until she was grown up. The girl is crying, and a woman says severely that she should not cry, because "everyone of us has gone through this."

Nde kulila tata wandi mayo mulenge	My father, come and help me
nde kulilaee	my mother come and help me
nde kwita mayo wandi	

My informants told me that the stone represents a crown, as the end of her education. Others said it is a heavy load on her head to symbolise her ordeal and need of help particularly from her parents. It is the role of the parents to liberate her from her ordeal. Therefore she has to call their names. She was mainly educated by her grandmother. Therefore her grandmother took the stone off the girl's head.

> The mother's sister has to dance, to show that she is happy that her daughter is mature now, and to show respect to the women and thank the women who have taught her daughter.

Nemwine mwana bane	Me, the mother of the girl,
chiwa mishee	I am very happy

> The *banacimbusa* tells the girl that she is an adult now, she must always be responsible and be aware of what she has learned, and use her common sense.

After this, the atmosphere changed, people are happy, dancing and drinking. They have finished their job.

The girl is covered under a blanket behind the *banacimbusa*, while they both leave the room. They come into the room again, walking normally. The girl is given another *citenge* now (not a new one).

She is allowed to have a bath. She can wash herself because she is a person, an individual now. After this she is dressed according to the norms of everyday life. She should have got new clothes but her relatives could not afford to pay for them. Usually the women wash the girl in the stream, but at this particular time the stream was dry so they had to leave this out.

The biological mother of the girl comes and helps the other women with the cooking of the chicken and other food. The food is ready, and everyone starts to eat.
After this, the girl and her *banacimbusa* are sitting outside, on a *citenge*, while all the people who have attended the initiation ritual speak to the girl to give her advice and some money. The money is partly for the *banacimbusa* and partly for the girl. When everyone has given the girl some advice, they leave.

A few neighbours are watching this from a distance, but they do not come closer. It seems that they are not allowed to come closer.

This shows that it is not a community happening, but a private rite.

After the ritual
After the rite, the girl has to learn the drawings, which were taught by the *banacimbusa* for a few days during two weeks. Hereafter she had to say all the meanings, as a test. The grandmother had to witness, so that she was sure that the *banacimbusa* had taught her granddaughter in a proper way. When the grandmother left the *banacimbusa* wanted to "check the girl's virginity", so she had to show her vulva. The girl did not want to do this, but the *banacimbusa* said: "You have to, do not be shy, you are still a girl and we are women." This was the first time (except for the very beginning of the rite) that the girl had to show her genitals. The *banacimbusa* told me that it was very impolite for adults to show their vulva, even in the initiation rite.

It shows that even after the initiation rite, the girl is still not a real woman. Initiation is the first step to womanhood and the first step to having more knowledge revealed and gaining further gradations of status.

It seems that there are less and less girls who have an initiation rite like this.
In the next chapter I will discuss the relevance of initiation rites in an urban environment today and what role the church plays in these rites.

6

Christian Women and Initiation Rites in an Urban Setting

In the previous I have described the initiation rite I attended on the Copperbelt. In the present chapter I will discuss the relevance of these rites in an urban environment today and analyse the role that the Catholic church can play in these rites.

Although Richards (1956, 134) claimed that the initiation rites are disappearing rather quickly, they are still performed, even in an urban and in a Roman Catholic setting. There are some changes in these rites, but the roots still exist. In urban settings the life of the people has changed. Despite or because of the heterogeneous groups in the Copperbelt and claims for ethnicity, there is a continuity and a continuance of values as expressed in rituals.

6.1. Changed circumstances and changed customs

In towns the social and moral order is different from what it used to be in the villages. Also the economic life has changed. Economically the relationship between husband and wife was based on interdependency and both of them had strictly prescribed duties. Today men are breadwinners and although many women are selling on the markets, they all claimed this to be additional. Domestic duties have more or less stayed the same. Besides, the husband is more conscious of his wife's economic dependence on him, and in urban areas women have commercial activities outside the house.

The pressure put on women, particularly by chairladies, about how to behave towards their husbands, shows that women do not behave according to what they have learnt. Chairladies try to keep the moral order. Although women say that they have to submit (for some this is really the case) in general they feel themselves strong. They are not passive and in need, but they are active, doing everything concerning to the house and are responsible for the children, partly because of the matrilineal system, partly because this is usually seen as women's work. There is a high solidarity among women.

Touwen (1984) claims that there are more and more female-headed households. Among my group of 39 informants, eleven were widows and seven were divorced, but seven of them were remarried. I agree with Touwen when she states that young women particularly want to remarry, because single women, either widowed or divorced, have a low status and they are looking for economic security for themselves and their children. Men are expected to behave along well-defined societal norms and a husband has to fulfil these obligations. Most of the elderly women did not want to remarry, because they were "old enough to be independent." (Touwen 1985, 44). This is what they also told me.

The bride service has made way for the bride price. In pre-colonial times, the bride service or later the bride price was about the same for every girl (Munachonga 1989, 292). It was a sign of respect and at the same time a sort of guarantee that the woman would be treated well. This bride price (*impango*) was paid by the husband only for his wife and did not put a claim on his future children. The bride price increased within the money economy. Nowadays the future husband has to pay for the education of the girl, which means that the parents of a well-educated girl will get more than the parents whose daughter is not educated. To pay for the education of the girl looks like "buying" the girl, according to Munachonga (1989, 292).

All women emphasised that a girl should be a virgin when she marries (see chapter 3). The fact that no one could tell me the word for virgin in Chibemba seems to me the evidence that virginity became important only recently, revealing the influence of Christianity and modern life.

There binary oppositions are waning, e.g. nowadays many unmarried and even uninitiated girls are having children (Van der Lans and Nooter 1988, 90), which makes the boundary between initiated and uninitiated less clear. The boundaries between young and old people and between married and unmarried persons are fading. The age of marriage has gone up for both sexes, due to education and the high cost of living. Girls want to experiment with their sexuality, and they have sexual relationships in exchange for money, presents or to pass exams at school and they have boyfriends. There is also a difference between being a church member or not, or being a Catholic or a member of another church. It is obvious that young women and men live in a different situation compared to their parents. They want to change compared to the lives of their parents, but also want to stick to the tradition. There is not really a new symbolic order. Hellman (1964, 347) claims that for the urban, there is a constant struggle to maintain or reaffirm standards or create new standards.

Changes have taken place regarding the widow-inheritance (*ubupiani*). Women's organisations object to this practice (see chapter 3). In 1989 a law was made according to which women are supposed to get a certain amount of the belongings of the spouse for the children and dependants. This law is unclear, not well known and often the relatives of the deceased do not obey this law. However, not every woman is willing to follow this law, because in this way she can easily be accused of having killed her husband by witchcraft, because she wanted to have his belongings. Also many women are protesting about the ritual cleansing. Because of the fear of AIDS people have developed alternatives such as ritually washing the woman's beads that she wears around her waist, giving white beads to the woman, or sleeping with each other without having sexual intercourse. The brother of the deceased is supposed to marry the widow, which means that he has to look after her. For a woman, this can give her financial security, but many women prefer to stay single or choose a new husband themselves. This too is sometimes explained as having used witchcraft, because she wanted to be single. From the point of view of tradition, it is good for a woman to receive someone who looks after her, but from a feminist point of view it is hard to be given to someone without a free choice. More and more men are refusing to marry or look after the sister-in-law mainly because of lack of money and the lesser bonds of kinship.

Also changes have taken place regarding marriages. There are many forms of marriage now, such as the marriage under ordinance and the church wedding. The customary marriage, which is based on African law and customs, still exists. Next to this, one can have marriage under the Marriage Act (ordinance marriage). The latter derives from European culture and was installed in 1964. Its features are: monogamy, validated by fulfilment of civil requirements, which frees the conjugal pair from control by the extended kin. It gives the woman rights to maintenance at divorce and the marriage is dissolved by death of a spouse, which gives a widow freedom to remarry. Women married under ordinance mostly belong to the small group of elite women. The greater part of women are married under customary law and therefore bound to customary regulations concerning divorce and inheritance (Touwen 19884, 18). Marriages are legal when all the essential requirements are satisfied. Consent by both parties is important; both the woman concerned and her parents have to give consent to the marriage. In addition, there are Catholic marriages. Only a few people have a Catholic marriage. E.g. in Luangwa there were 181 Catholic marriages in the period from 1982 to 1992, and 120 Catholic marriages between 1977 and 1982. All couples had a traditional wedding first, and after some time, often after a few years, they had a church wedding. This small number of Catholic church weddings is due to the fact that this wedding does not recognise a divorce.

The people in Luangwa said that marriage means a customary marriage, usually arranged by the parents, with the payment of a bride price. However, many (young) people did not have a marriage of this kind, but arranged a wedding themselves without paying a bride price or did not arrange anything. Despite this they considered themselves to be married.

Richards (1940, 23) claims that companionship between man and wife is in fact a happy accident in Bemba society, not the universal ambition of every boy and girl. In my research in an urban setting both boys and girls want to choose their partner. They indicate that it is not according to the tradition, but "it is better to choose your own partner, because then you are more or less sure that you love one another", although they all said the parents should agree with their choice and a bride price should be paid. Here we see the changed ideas about marriage, influenced by Christianity and a western way of living, although it is still not fully accepted.

The association of the *chisungu* and the ritual purification of the couple (see chapter three) has weakened. According to my (female) informants only men did not want to keep this ritual purification. The ritual cleaning could be refused when a husband had committed adultery, thus to refuse it could be seen as a punishment by a woman. Couples are less likely to attribute their misfortunes to the breaking of ritual sanctions (Jules-Rosette 1980, 394). Exclusiveness of the sexual bond between partners is disappearing (Hellman 1964, 350). The old sanctions have lost their force and the sanctions which regulate urban life are not yet applicable.

However, initiation rite continues to be recognised by both young and older people as an important event which they claim has not changed substantially despite its curtailment. This shortening makes it possible to maintain the rite in an urban environment and does not entirely represent a turn away from ritual.

6.2. Ritual in an urban setting

All rites must be seen in their social context. In chapter four it was said that rituals are a comment on the society and are performed to clearify some problems or tensions. In this way the initiation rite can be interpreted. Girls are brought up in a male-dominated society which at the same time is matrilineal organised. Fathers are respected, but the ultimate power lies with the mother's brother. The honouring of the future husband enacts the desire of women to attract men; in the past to stay with them in the matrilocal village, today to stay with them in town. The women court men to give them children, but deny them the full rights of a sociological father. The denying of power over his children may be compensated in the initiation rite by giving him much respect (Richards 1956, 159). I agree with Richards, who suggests that there is a connection between the lack of open hostility between the genders and the unconscious feeling of guilt at robbing the man of his children. This is expressed in fears of the women that men will leave them, and men saying that their wives will not respect them unless they are taught to do so in initiation rite (Richards 1956, 160).

Ritual is the product of a more or less conflicted social reality; a process within which an attempt is made to impress a dominant message upon a set of paradoxical or discordant representations (Comaroff 1985, 119).

From a materialist point of view, Van Binsbergen (1981, 219) states that people are operating in three structurally different and geographically segregated segments: the village, the networks in the urban settings and the formal urban organisations. Urban ritual, however much reminiscent of the village, can not be explained by reference to the rural structure (Van Binsbergen 1981, 221). Ritual is an occasion to build up social credit as is necessary for survival. Any ritual seems to be capable of providing organisational devices for this purpose.

Symbolism and ritual sanctions have subjective reality in that they function at the participant's level, and precisely because the participant is unaware of the economic background of urban ritual participation. The imputed references of ritual, e.g. claims to assistance in future need, become disguised in the ritual process, but these disguises become a subjective reality for the participants, and this subjective reality begins to pattern their behaviour more or less in its own right (Van Binsbergen 1981, 227). This is an intermediate, relatively autonomous level of functioning of ritual symbolism and sanctions. Thus ritual is used to shape social relations. The central issues in present-day ritual are not so much impersonal beliefs and values, but power and competition over social relationships which provide access to scarce resources. Ritual interpretations are constantly shifted, new ones are invented and the rules of the ritual are largely determined not by immutable custom, but by the individual specialist (Van Binsbergen 1981, 230). This comes close to the "invention of tradition" and can be illustrated with the arguments the women had while performing the rite (see chapter five).

Van Binsbergen (1985, 216) states that the economically insecure urbanites seek to create a basis of solidarity so that they may appeal to each other when they are in need. Any ritual, including initiation rites, can serve this purpose. Here the church also can provide a setting for the construction of alternative kin solidarity in town and tries to influence the contents of the ritual as well.

6.3. Community and ethnicity

In towns the bonds of kinship were loosening and the influence of elders was waning (Richards 1939, 403). In this vacuum the church tries to take the place of the kinship or community, where ethical principles are enforced. West (1975), who has conducted field-research in South Africa, claims that the church does not work along ethnic lines. The Catholic church aspires to universalism and to be for everyone.

There is still the problem of ethnicity. Although it is known that initiation rites are more or less the same for every ethnic group, people still claim them to be specific for one ethnic group. However, Jules-Rosette (1980, 394) mentions the initiation of Bemba girls by Cewa women. My informants said there are also people from other ethnic groups who have their daughter initiated by Bemba women after their own initiation, if they can afford it. They claimed this was because there are many mixed marriages now, so they should know the customs of another ethnic group as well. The initiation I attended was performed by Bemba women. Only the chairlady came from Luapula, and was a Ngombo, a group who claimed to be Bemba. Among the Nazarethi *banacimbusa* there were two women who were not Bemba. They were not present during the rite. The reasons they gave were that they had to go a funeral. I do not know whether this was true. My informants claimed that when one of the helpers does not belong to the same ethnic group as the girl concerned, they still attend the ritual, but leave some specific things out, and just do the "general things", which are common in most ethnic groups. As initiation rites for different ethnic groups have much in common, this is not so difficult in practice. Since the church is poly-ethnic, one can expect the ritual performed by church women, to be poly-ethnic as well. However, it is still an item that needs more research.

6.4. The Catholic church and initiation rites

The church has changed its point of view and does not condemn the initiation rite any longer. On the contrary, due to the renewal in the church after the Vatican Council II, indigenous rituals are revalued.

The missionaries now recognise that they have misinterpreted many traditional customs, including initiation rites and are dealing with enculturation. This is a theoretical view, instigated by the renewals in the Catholic church. In practice it is different.

The church wants to combine initiation rites with Christian values, so they will be "Christian initiation rites". Priests want to combine initiation with rituals in church. There are many rituals in the Catholic church, of which Confirmation, the ritual in which young people confirm to be a member of the Catholic church, seems to fit best, because it usually takes place at the age of puberty. Priests are trying to take part in and change the rites, but up till now without success. Among the eight priests I interviewed, only one European priest was really trying to get involved in initiation rites, but did not succeed. This priest organised separate seminars for girls and boys for Confirmation. During these seminars, women teach girls traditional things about sexuality. Parents of the girls concerned complained about it, because they said girls should not be taught in this way and the teaching should be kept outside the church. One other priest, the one mentioned in chapter five, wanted to get involved in initiation rites and to Christianise them, but without success, because women did not want to tell him about initiation. The other European and the African priests I interviewed hardly tried to get involved in initiation rites. They all said that initiation rites should be Christianised, but it had certainly not a priority. The European sisters wanted to get involved in initiation rites and enculturation, but hardly have a say in it. The Zambian sisters, who all had experienced an initiation rite (one just after the onset of menstruation, two when they wanted to enter the religious order) said initiation rites were good, but it would even be better to combine them with prayers.

In general, the European priests said initiation rites were useless for women, because women were only taught to be subservient and these rites are irrelevant, because girls are taught things they can not practice in town, such as agriculture. They often said that the good things should be kept, while the bad things should be left out. However, they hardly managed to mention which things they considered to be good and thought most of the African values are negative for women. They said in initiation the girls should learn about a happy marriage, which means a marriage based on love and understanding, and there should be a dialogue between husband and wife. For this purpose the priest who organises seminars for Confirmation, has also made a programme for women to teach *banacimbusas* about Christian marriage and initiation rites. This programme is used in the congregation where this priest works. It shows the interpretation of initiation rites by the priest (see Appendix B).

The church wants to implement Christian values, and has the authority to do so. The church can be seen as an educational institute. Although it is hardly involved in initiation rites, it prepares would-be spouses by pre-marital training performed by priests, nuns and catechists. In this training they teach about love for each other, taking care of the future children, and how to financially monitor the marriage.

New organisations such as Marriage Encounter and the Family Life Movement, which are based on Catholic concepts, teach the same. The members of these organisations are well-educated. The purpose of these organisations is to stimulate a dialogue between husband and wife, as equals (in addition to childspacing, which is the main purpose of the Family Life Movement). They also try to instigate discussions between mothers and daughters and fathers and sons about sexual education. Their argument is that because of the high amount of premarital sexual relationships and the increase of AIDS and STD (Sexually Transmitted Diseases), parents should prepare or warn their children. To some extent this seems to be necessary and helpful, but it is counter to the culture.

It seems that people want or need this and that it is a way to create order in the new social life in town. It shows that the nuclear family is more and more important, and that the extended family is waning (Jonker 1992, 230). Here the church also uses its influence, and tries to change customs, or actually takes advantage of the changes which are going on.

Women's initiation rites in a Christian way focus on domestic responsibilities and are structurally linked primarily to the family rather than to the community at large (Jules-Rosette 1980, 405). The emergence of women's initiation rites in association with churches suggests an attempt to hold the domestic circle intact by retaining critical aspects of the women's traditional status. Despite new pressure toward autonomy and occupational diversification, the church emphasises the continuing importance of the bride's virginity and her contribution as a producer of offspring. In this way women's initiation rite becomes a vehicle of preservation in conditions of social flux. While it is difficult to maintain a close-knit, traditional community in a town setting, the family unit can be sustained.

A ritual can serve many masters (Pina Cabral 1992, 53). Therefore Catholic women can perform the rite, and it can be performed in a Catholic way. The women's groups, in particular the Nazarethi, aim at revitalising the traditional initiation rite, because it is seen as the basis of a good marriage and a happy family life. The Nazarethi, which was founded on the Copperbelt and has groups all over Zambia now, focus particularly on family life and emphasise the values of the relationship between husband and wife and discuss education of children. Priests are rather negative about the Nazarethi, because they only perform traditional initiation rites and do not teach Christian values.

6.5. Women's views on initiation rites

The most frequently given answer to the question why they perform traditional initiation rites while at the same time they are Christians was "Initiation has nothing to do with the church." Often they added: "but we teach the same."

This means that there is a gap between the church and the culture. Women do not want priests or other men to be involved, and they want to keep it separated from the church. It is their tradition while the church is rather new. There are also similarities between initiation and Christianity. These are mainly pre-Christian values, such as not stealing, not committing adultery.

The reasons the women gave for performing an initiation rite were that girls should learn good manners and not socialise with boys. The initiation rite is the best way to teach, "because it is the way it has always been done." Actually the best way to teach is by showing the *mbusa,* by singing the songs which they repeat many times during the ritual and by miming. However, the *mbusa* are hardly used any more. Only two girls among the eleven girls I spoke with, claimed that the *mbusa* were used in their initiation rite, the others claimed that they would be shown at the wedding ceremony.

All the women and girls said the initiation rite was a good, albeit hard time but was necessary to learn the most important things of life. Initiation for women is their way to feel strong, adult, to have self-reliance and is a good preparation for marriage. Other reasons for performing the rite are that parents are afraid of having their daughter sent back after marriage or that the future husband will reclaim the bride price, in case the woman had not had a proper initiation rite. Many claimed that a marriage will be successful only when the woman has been initiated and that divorces are due to the fact that the young woman was not initiated, so she does not know how to look after her husband. This is also mentioned by Chondoka (1988) and Jules-Rosette (1980, 394). Another reason is that an uninitiated woman can easily be accused of being a witch, because she is an outsider. She is still in the "cold" world. She will be kept outside the women's world, and is called a *cipelelo,* someone who has not learned. Another motive is that women have the authority to practise the rites and use their authority to make the girl a member of the community. In initiation the girl is "made a woman", so this process of socialisation has to do with the social construction of womanhood.

Among the women I interviewed, only one said initiation rites should be combined with Christianity. She was the grandmother of the girl who's initiation rite I described in chapter five. This is a reason why the priest was allowed during a part of the initiation, although the women performing the rite said they did not want him to be there. His presence was exceptional. They only showed him the *mbusa* while the girl was not in the same room. They did not show him everything and did not want him to attend, because it is a women's item, for and with women only.

6.6. Christian *banacimbusas*

Traditionally a *banacimbusa* is regarded as a wise woman and treated with respect. She has knowledge about traditional customs and teaches girls during their initiation rites. She is a traditional midwife who is of irreproachable conduct, who has undergone an initiation rite and a traditional wedding ceremony, has delivered children and has a stable marriage. She used to assist a young woman she had initiated at the delivery of her first child. Although this is not always possible today, it is still preferable. If possible, she is still the one who teaches the young mother how to look after the baby. The *banacimbusa* is the first one to go to in case of problems and all women said they show her respect. The *banacimbusas* indeed said that the majority of the girls they had initiated visited them regularly. If they did not, this was because they lived far away.

To become a *banacimbusa* is more and more the privilege of church group members. Although this title is a traditional one, it is also used for women whose authority to teach girls is derived from the church. They are thus a new sort of *banacimbusa*. Today all the *banacimbusas* are a member of a church lay group, particularly of the Nazarethi. All *banacimbusas* are married in church. All the chairladies of the women's groups are *banacimbusa*, so these women have multiplex roles. Since the church is important in the urban area, people want a Christian *banacimbusa* for their daughter, which they claimed to be more reliable than a non-Christian. Here the influence of the network of the women's church group is clear.

The question is whether they want to teach Christian values, because in the initiation rite nothing is told about Christianity, and all claimed that they wanted to keep their tradition. Christianity and culture are complementary. The power of the chairladies gives them self-esteem. The combination of being a *banacimbusa* and a chairlady provides authority. Women used the church to get authority, which they can use to perform the rites, and now the church tries to use these women to perform the rites in a Christian way.

The Catholic women in Luangwa are well-informed about the Old Testament, in which there are many similarities with their own culture, e.g.: parents choosing partners for their children (Gen. 20:12, 24:4, 15, 29, 28:2; Num. 36:8), the bride price, the idea that having many children is a gift from God (Gen. 24:60; Ps 127:3), polygamy (Gen. 4:19), levirate and taking the name of a deceased (Deut. 25:5-10; Ruth 4:10; Gen. 16:1-3).

They are also familiar with the New Testament. From a theological point of view, it can be said that by being a Christian the *banacimbusa* is the link between the culture and the church. The *banacimbusa* is knowledgeable about the culture, the ritual and the secret emblems which are given by the ancestors. In this way they may be seen as priests.

A parallel between the tradition and Christianity is that the *banacimbusa* will be the godmother (*bemininchi* both male and female) of the girl's first child, and sometimes of the following children as well, when they are baptised in church. The godfather of a boy is the husband of the *banacimbusa*. The *banacimbusa* leads the wedding ceremony of the girl she has initiated, and when the girl is marrying in church, the *banacimbusa* will be the witness, and her husband will be the witness for the man. The ideal is, that it is the same *banacimbusa* who has initiated the girl who takes these Christian roles, but in practice this is not always possible. In these cases, another *banacimbusa* will be witness or godmother.

In conformity with traditional views, the *banacimbusa* is the second mother of the girl. She can discuss all kinds of things, even sexual problems. According to the Christian values the godmother is the second mother. This means that the *banacimbusa* has traditional tasks in traditional ceremonies and Christian tasks in Christian ceremonies as well. This is another parallel between the tradition and Christianity.

There is a wish for the fulfilment of the marriage. The *banacimbusa* has gone through all the phases; she has gone all the way from a proper initiation rite, a proper wedding ceremony, has given birth to some children, lives according to traditional values and has become a *banacimbusa* and has had a church wedding. Thus the *banacimbusa* is three in one: she represents tradition, she is a traditional teacher and a Christian.

From a Christian point of view women can enhance their position. The *banacimbusa* can have an important role in this through initiation rite. The *banacimbusa* can play an important role to teach Christianity and enhance the position of women. This can be illustrated with the remark a chairperson of a church group made to the members: "The Bible is your *banacimbusa*."

6.7. The continuation of initiation rites in the context of a church

Changes in the ritual may be imposed by outside authorities; spontaneous developments are quickly assimilated to the ideal fixed form and given the sanction of long tradition (Cohen 1985, 17). This can also be seen in the initiation rite for girls on the Copperbelt. Although there have been many changes in this rite, due to factors of time, social factors, the area that changed from village to town and because it is not written down, the main practices are still the same and the people who perform the rite claim it to be very old.

The continuation of the rite is a reassertion of the continued importance of women's socio-economic contribution in a radically changing environment. The ambivalence embodied in the rites as reminders of custom and indicators of change is incontestable (Jules-Rosette 1980, 404).

Ritual is a symbolic expression of both change and commitment, and of change and continuity (Cohen 1985, 96). This can also be seen in the rites on the Copperbelt. Rites maintain common values and reaffirm norms in relation to the contemporary situation (Turner 1957, 317).

According to Moore (1977, 212) rituals are representations of fixed social reality, of continuity. People try to control their situations by trying to fix social reality, to give it form and order.

The reasons for continuing the performances of initiation rites are that children must learn, which mean be socialised, and that traditions must be passed from one generation to the next. But in the urban environment ritual becomes mixed with new and other elements. It becomes a mixture, a *bricolage*. The *bricolage* of the ritual by the women in Luangwa can be seen as a way to reform the world in the image they have created to re-establish a correspondence between the self and the structures that contain it.

Ritual bridges the gap between experience and social ideas (Cohen 1985, 92; Jules-Rosette 1981, 198). The disruption caused by social change might be seen as a particular instance of disjunction between the ideal and the actual: one in which the ideal takes the guise of the familiar and actuality appears as the unfamiliar and therefore the feared or resented.

Cohen (1985, 91-92) writes:

"(...) fantasy (...) permits deeply entrenched customary symbolic forms to be used in radically changed circumstances. It thereby manages change so that it limits the disruption of people's orientations to their community, and enables them to make sense of novel circumstances through the use of familiar idioms."

In the rite in town the aspects of ideal and fantasy construction of their world are clear. Initiation rites emphasise reproductive and domestic productive roles for women and respect for authority, while urban women have different tasks today and they have hardly any ties with a village and have various sexual relationships.

The shortening of the rites implies that many things are omitted, such as the items about magical instructions and working in the fields. However, the instruction for three days may replace the half-year process, but it does not diminish the symbolic importance of the rites. Initiation involves the transfer of knowledge and expertise from one generation to another through the preparation of the initiates in sexual, familiar and broader social responsibilities and includes the major structural markers that designate phases of the individual life cycle. The rite of passage is still marking the transition from one stage to another, from child to womanhood. A girl needs to go through this process, to be a full member of the community. It is a way to be regarded as mature and to be respected by the community.

The church can not do this, because it does not have the traditional knowledge and authority. Initiation rites continue to be performed by women, to confirm their power and knowledge, and to introduce girls into the women's world.

Conclusion

In this book the central question was:

What do rites of passage mean for urban women and how are women who participate in women's church groups involved in rites of passage?

Subsidiary questions were:
- By what authority do Christian women perform initiation rites?
- What does the clergy think about initiation rites, as opposed to popular opinion?
- What is the relevance of initiation rites in towns?

In chapter one I have discussed the method of research to get an answer to these questions. In chapter two I have described the urban Copperbelt and the organisation of the Catholic church in Luangwa. In town the structure people need, is hardly to be found. The church tries to create a community by installing Christian communities. They exist only in parts of Luangwa, and do not work out. Women's church groups play an important role in the lives of women and give them structure to cope with problems they have in town. In these groups subservience is emphasised, while in the initiation rite a girl learns to be subservient, but also to be respected and to be self-reliant.

Initiation rites can be seen as the expression of fundamental social values, which I have explained in chapter three. The focus is on relations established by marriage, the community and its continuity in space and across the generations. Ritual is conceived of as the property of the ancestors, the founders of all social life. It must be handed on. Initiation rites create solidarity among women; it creates a community of women. The secret knowledge of initiation may be seen as a compensation for women from the seclusion of other aspects of life.

In chapter four I have stated that the rite is not so much concerned with the initiate, but with the community, confirming its structure and order. Initiation rites form a common corpus of knowledge among women and contribute to their solidarity as mature co-contributors to their families and communities.

The geographical change of the initiation rite, from village to town, may seem out of place and irrelevant. The traditional world-view and boundaries are not the same as in town. Initiation gives an illusion of reality, of the structure of the olden days in the village. Women claim to perform a Bemba rite, which shows that the illusion exists that the Bemba village was good and peaceful, and this illusion provides a message and direction for the rite. But the villages have changed. Besides, many people in South-Central Africa have more or less the same rite. Although the society has changed, people try to maintain the moral order. Ritual unites people. In towns, initiation rites continue to be essential for symbolising the young woman's transition to full adulthood.

In Luangwa the rites become more and more private today. Even the "showing of the girl", which used to be a celebration for many relatives and all people in the village, has almost disappeared. This more private character of the rite can be explained by the lack of kinsmen in the urban environment and the lack of a cohesive community, such as a village.

Initiation rites can work to build up a community. This means that it can work to (re)define boundaries. The oppositions in social life are abstract. Therefore symbols and rites of passage are needed to pass the boundary, which is needed to maintain the social order. Through initiation the boundary is made clear and through experiencing the initiation rite, a girl gets the right to pass the border. This boundary is a social construction and is important to keep the social order, to become a good ancestor, to keep the ancestral law. The border between young/old, male/female, married/unmarried, power/no power, child/adult, cold (outside society)/ hot (inside society) has to be maintained. To be a virgin until marriage is another way to keep boundaries and social order.

In the Catholic part of the township Luangwa, the women who conduct initiation rites have gained their authority not only because of their experience in ritual initiations and by their irreproachable conduct, but because they are members of a women's church group and have been married in church. The church wedding is a pre-condition for becoming a *banacimbusa*. Hence this is a new sort of *banacimbusa*. Thus women use the church to get authority, and now the church tries to use these women to Christianise initiation rites.

This is a remarkable change, because in the past, the initiation rite was condemned by the missionaries and the women who performed it were punished. The changed view of the church must be seen in the light of the Vatican Council II, in which it was stipulated that indigenous customs should be re-evaluated and revalued. Priests are trying to take part in the rites in order to change them, but up till now without success. Christian women continue to perform initiation rite in a traditional way.

Although the number of priests and sisters I interviewed is small, I think that in general priests have not really changed their opinion about initiation rites. In general, they still have a negative attitude towards the contents of initiation rites, and consider them to be oppressive for women. Although initiation rite contain elements one could call oppressive, there is more to it. It is the acquisition of regimens, the learning of habits, based on harmony with the spouse, parents(-in-law), older people in general, and mastering of conflicts. It is also the teaching of the proper attitudes toward the girl's gender role. They can also be seen as the passing on of knowledge and values such as harmony between husband and wife, based on (sexual) interdependency and harmony between young and old people, as I have shown in chapter five.

In the urban area of the Copperbelt people mingle, and they also mingle in women's church groups. Although women claim initiation rites to be specific for particular ethic groups, they are performed by people from different ethnic origin. This problem of ethnicity and initiation rites in a church context requires further study.

Experiencing the initiation rite is passing the border. Therefore a woman who does not experience initiation will stay on one side of the border, and is considered as an outsider, a *cipelelo*. She is kept outside the women's world. She has not learnt things that women are supposed to know in a way that they are supposed to learn. This indicates that the construction of womanhood is related to socialisation and the inertia of culture. Initiation rite is a means to the social construction of womanhood. The construction of womanhood is such a profound process that alien rituals, for instance those used by the church, are insufficiently powerful to bring about the notions that produce identity (Van Binsbergen 1994, 9).

Further and longer research is required into the subject of initiation rites in town and particularly in a Catholic context, as to provide for a deeper analysis. By the limited size of this book, I could only give an impulse to discuss and analyse this subject.

In chapter five I have described a non-Christian initiation rite, which was encapsulated within a church context. It might be hypothesised that the attempted construction of community involved is that of a moral community which is viable because it combines the symbolic potency of a local rural tradition with the organisational power and prestige of a world religion (Van Binsbergen 1994, 9).

The wish of women to keep initiation rites separate from the church, may be seen as a way to keep their autonomy. If the church really takes over this rite and changes it in a Christian way, it will be men who get involved and have a say in it.

Initiation rite still marks the transition from one stage to another, from child to womanhood. A girl needs to go through this process, to be a full member of the community. It is a way to be regarded as mature and to be respected by the community.

Initiation by the church does not work, because it does not have the rite in which the girl pass the boundary. A church rite can add something, but in practice it wants to leave the most important things out. A church rite does not create order; it may even create disorder when priests are involved.

By passing through the rite of passage, a woman can pass the knowledge and the rite of passage on to the next generation. Changing the rite by the church means that the rite is not passed on the way it should be done. Rites of passage continue to be performed by women, to confirm their autonomy and knowledge, and to introduce girls into the women's world.

Appendix A. Questionnaires

1. Questionnaire for the women's groups.

1) Can your group support the improvement of the social position of women?
2) How can women who participate in the group, at the same time be involved in initiation rites?
3) How do they defend such involvement, and what are their motives?
4) What authority do Christian women have to perform initiation rites?
5) What are the relations with the grown-up girls in the church?
6) Do girls learn about their rights during initiation?
7) Which right do they have now, and which rights did they have in the olden days?
8) How have initiation rites changed under the influence of church policy and how because of socio-economical changes?
9) What do you teach your daughters, and what do you teach your sons?
10) If an unmarried girl gets pregnant, is the girl, the mother or the boy to be blamed? Why?
11) Does an unmarried mother gets a lower bride price or a higher bride price, because she has a child already?
12) If two people want to get married, what is the bride price a man has to pay?
13) Does your husband look after his children, or after the children of his sister?
14) What do you do when your husband comes home late at night?
15) What do you do when your husband does not give you enough money although you know he earns enough to give you?
16) What do you do when your husband beats you?
17) What do you do when your husband wants to meet you, but you do not want to get pregnant?
18) If you have a problem, do you go to your *banacimbusa*, your friends, your relatives, your husbands' relatives, your group or others?
19) How is or was your relationship with your *banacimbusa*?
20) Is there much companionship among women? Do you have many friends?

2. Questions for interviews with women.

1) In which women's group are you?
2) Why are you a member of particularly this group?
3) What does the group do to improve the position of women?
4) Are there one or more *banacimbusas* in your group?
5) What do you think of initiation rites?
6) How can you perform initiation rites when you are a Christian?
7) What do girls learn in initiation rites?
8) Did you have an initiation rite yourself? When and where?
9) How long was your initiation rite?
10) How have initiation rites changed from the past?
11) Why do people want initiation rites to be performed by church women?
12) Do you go to the meetings of the Christian community?
13) What do you think of the Christian community?
14) What is more important to you: the women's group or the Christian community?

3. Questionnaires for priests.

1) Are there women's groups in your parish?
2) How can these groups enhance the position of women?
3) What do you think about enculturation?
4) What do you think about initiation rites for girls?
5) Do you want to change these rites into Christian initiation rites?
6) Are there women in your parish who prepare girls for a Christian initiation or a Christian wedding?
7) Are there many girls or parents who want to have a Christian initiation or a church wedding?
8) Are there Christian communities in your parish?
9) Are they working well?
10) What are the reasons that they work well or that they do not work?
11) Are there many men attending the meetings of the Christian communities?
12) Are the chairpersons male or female?

4. Questionnaires for Youfra girls.

1) Do you know girls who are grown-up but not initiated?
2) What do you think of these girls?
3) What do you think is best: if you choose your own future husband or if your parents choose him?
4) Did you have an initiation rite? When and where?
5) How many women helped the *banacimbusa* during your initiation rite?

6) Did they show you the clay models and drawings?
7) How long did you stay inside the house?
8) How many days was the teaching?
9) Did you feel mentally grown-up after your initiation rite?
10) What do you think of people who are getting married without paying a bride price?
11) When is a woman a real woman: when she has had her initiation rite, when she is grown-up without having an initiation rite, when she is married or when she has a child?
12) Did you have a Christian initiation rite?
13) Is your *banacimbusa* a Catholic?
14) Is one of your brothers or sisters married to a son or daughter of your *banacimbusa*?
15) Who wanted them to marry?
16) Do you think that Christian women have a say about you?
17) Is there companionship among women, do you feel companionship for women?
18) Will your *banacimbusa* be the same *banacimbusa* at your wedding ceremony and at the delivery of your first child? Would you like this?
19) Why do not many people have a wedding ceremony nowadays?
20) What do you think of people who are married without a wedding ceremony?
21) Would you like to have a traditional wedding ceremony when you are getting married?
22) Would you like to marry in church?
23) What do you think about girls who have a sexual relationship before marriage?
24) What do you think about sexual abuse by boys, teachers, fathers, grandfathers? Does this happen often?
25) Why do girls marry late, when they are twenty years or older?

Appendix B.   Christian Marriage Preparation Programme

Marriage preparation programme using traditional marriage values and Christian values.

<u>Instructions for teachers for marriage preparations.</u>

1- It is a rich time to instruct the bride. Do not forget to mention that you are Christian and teach Christian values. It should keep the couple to have a good marriage in future. Strengthen their love for each other.

- When you teach do not only follow what was taught long time ago, traditionally. Teach what is good in this instruction, but keep in account the present day circumstances.

2- As the girl is an adult, teach her as an adult. Do not think that she knows nothing. Teach her only respectable matters.

3- The man is the head of the household, but he is not a boss.

- The wife is not the slave of the husband. The wife is his beloved.

4- Teaching her that she should keep a small broom near the bed so that that she starts sweeping when her husband is angry is teaching her to despise her husband.

What is needed in the house is mutual understanding, mutual love to make each other . happy, to work together, to talk together.

Both husband and wife should be taught that it is good to talk together. At other times it is good to be silent.

- To teach a girl that she should be the first one to be up in the morning, that she should kneel down for her husband or clap in her hands when he comes is not teaching her to love one another.

They should learn how to greet each other, to welcome each other, not only one should do this.

- The wife is not the slave of the husband. Both should help each other if they want to have a good marriage, not one should be good in governing the other. They should know from each other what the other needs.

- Do not insult the girl or make her suffer. You should not beat her or pinch her.

- Midwives sometimes undress the girls. Why? There is no use for.
- Do the ceremony with the chicken, but tell her where it leads to.
- You should keep in account that if you do the ceremony on a Saturday night, people will be drunk on Sunday morning and disturb church services. Why not do the ceremonies on Friday evening and go on on Saturdays. This makes less disturbance in the village or in the town.

5- The marriage act should make both husband and wife happy. Let each one give the other what he or she needs to be happy. As Saint Paul says in Kor. 7, 3-5: "The husband must give to his wife what she has the right to expect and so too the wife to the husband."

- Do not teach the girl she should have slavery manners towards her husband. It looks as if only the wife must make the man happy. How can a man be happy if he sees the wife is only a slave?
- It is difficult to ensure if the girl is a virgin. The membrane might have been broken even if she has not slept with a man.
- You can tell the girl the customs from earlier times about the marriage pot, only explain it to her.
- If you teach her about intercourse do not tell her: "do not do this, do not do that". Leave those instructions, so that they do what pleases them, provided they show each other love and have an affability for each other. Teach them things which make them happy. Do not teach things which makes them afraid.

6- To break taboos. Many people think that when a woman menstruates she must do not do this or that, but she does not defile anybody. She can cook, she can put salt in the relish, she can close a door, she can do all those things, she can also take a child of another person in her arms. If you want her to rest from time to time, let her husband help her sometimes.

Do not teach about *ncila* or *ncentu* (unfaithfulness, adultery).

Teach her how to respect her husband, teach her not to desire others, to be faithful. If she is unfaithful, she cheats her husband and she damages their mutual love. But leave out those instructions about the charms of adultery.

7- According to the customs, the wife should clean the husband and the husband should clean the wife and they should shave each other. There is nothing wrong in this, as long as both of them wish to do it this way. Do not shave the bride to prepare her for marriage. She is an adult so she can ask for help if she wants to shave or clean herself. You should not decide that it is your work.

8- The maternal aunt should bring the bride and receive some money, but she should not receive money that day. It should be arranged so that you will receive the money another day, otherwise you give the girl the impression that she is bought.

You should not remain to ensure that the marital act has taken place. You will make the man anxious and he might fail because you are there. You will leave them alone and it will be secret what happened. If they experience any difficulties, then they have the time to talk things over and to diminish the difficulties.

9- One should be respectful to the in-laws, but they should not fear them. They should be received as their children. The instruction of fearing the in-laws is not Christian.

10- Teach the girl to show happiness. The duty that the girl should show sadness is not necessary. It is imposed.

11- In the house, after the wedding you should leave the instructions of what they must do to the couple. Bring them food once, but they should not be forbidden to talk together. Let them do as they please.

What to instruct

1 Respect towards each other.
2 Dialogue; each one will have his time to speak or to be quiet.
3 If you pinch the husband he will not be docile.
4 Money is from both, for both.
5 To restrict imposed isolation.

To teach the husband

1 You are not the boss, not the chief. Your wife is not your slave or your employee. She is your beloved.
2 The house belongs to both of you. The money is for both of you.
3 Respect and to respect each other.
4 To talk together and to judge together. This is the medicine for a good marriage.

Glossary

banacimbusa	traditional midwife, mentrix
bemininchi	godmother, both male and female
cena chisungu	female tree, usually used in initiation rites (*mubwilili*)
chisungu	girls' initiation rite
cipelelo	someone who does not keep the rules
citenge	cloth
citongo	someone who has not learned, who is not initiated
citente	Christian or basic community
fitenge	plural of *citenge*
fitente	plural of *citente*
insaka ya parish	Parish Council
kabungwe kabalanda	committee for the poor
kafwa	helper, chairperson
kwingisha shifyala	ritual of the acceptance of the son-in-law
Mabumba	women's church group
maka	law, jurisdiction, or duty
mbusa	sacred emblems, clay models and drawings
mipashi ya ifikolwe	prayer to the ancestors
mubwilili tree	female tree, usually used in initiation rites (*cena chisungu*)
mufungu tree	tree used in initiation rites, both male and female
mupundu tree	tree used in initiation rites, it bears sweet fruits
nachabindwa	taboo
nachisungu	the initiate
ncentu	adultery, committed by a wife
ncila	adultery, committed by a husband
nsambu	right or duty
nshima	main nutriment, made of pounded maize
ubupiani	ritual to clean the last-living spouse from the spirit of the deceased
ukucilo mukashi	to jump over someone's spirit; to mix blood

Bibliography

BEATTIE, J.H.M. (1970), On understanding ritual. In: Wilson B. (ed.), *Rationality*. Oxford: Basil Blackwell. pp 240-268.

CARMODY, P.B. (1988), Conversion to Roman Catholicism in Zambia. Shifting pedagogies. *African Christian Studies*, vol. *4*, no. *2*. June 1988. pp 5-21.

CHONDOKA, Y.A. (1988), *Traditional marriages in Zambia*. Ndola (Zambia): Mission Press.

COHEN, A.P. (1985), *The symbolic construction of community*. London: Tavistock Publications.

COMAROFF, J. (1985), *Body of power, spirit of resistance*. Chicago: University of Chicago Press.

CORBEIL, J.J. (1982), *Mbusa; sacred emblems of the Bemba*. Mbala (Zambia): Moto Moto Museum, London: Ethnographic Publishers.

DONDEYNE, A. (1967), De juiste bevordering van de culturele vooruitgang. In: *Vaticanum 2. De kerk in de wereld van deze tijd. Schema dertien, tekst en commentaar*. Hilversum: Uitgeverij Paul Brand. pp 148-166.

DOUGLAS, M. (1966), *Purity and danger: An analysis of the concepts of pollution and taboo*. London: Routledge.

EPSTEIN, A.L. (1958), *Politics in an urban African community*. Manchester: University press.

— (1964), Conflict and growth in the urban community (1940-50). In: Eisenstadt, S.N. (ed.), *Comparative social problems*. New York: The Free Press. pp 351-369.

— (1978), *Ethos and identity*. London: Tavistock Publications.

— (1981), *Urbanisation and kinship: The domestic domain on the Copperbelt of Zambia 1950-1956*. London: Academic Press.

FLANNERY, A. (1975), *Vatican Council II*, A. Flannery (ed.). Tenbury Wells (England): Fowler Wright Books Ltd.

GAITSKELL, D. (1990), Devout domesticity? A century of African women's Christianity in South Africa. In: *Women and Gender in Southern Africa to 1945*. London: James Curry Ltd. pp 251-272.

GARVEY B. (1977), Bemba chiefs and Catholic missions. *Journal of History, 3*. pp 411-426.

GAYOMALI, J. (1990), *Reshaping a Zambian community: Situation, vision and organization of the Christian community of Luangwa*. Kitwe (Zambia): St. Maximilian Kolbe Catholic Parish. (unpublished)

GESCHIERE, P. (1985), Imposing capitalist dominance through the state: The multifarious of the colonial state in Africa. In: Van Binsbergen, W.M.J. and P. Geschiere (eds.), *Old modes of production and capitalist encroachment*. London: Kegan Paul International Ltd. pp 94-143.

GESCHIERE, P. AND R. RAATGEVER (1985), Introduction: Emerging insights and issues in French marxist anthropology. In: Van Binsbergen, W.M.J. and P. Geschiere (eds.), *Old modes of production and capitalist encroachment*. London: Kegan Paul International Ltd. pp 1-38.

GLUCKMAN, M. (1962), Les Rites De Passage. In: Gluckman, M. (ed.), *Essays on the ritual of social relations*. Manchester: University Press.

HACKETT, R.I.J. (1990), "Women no Saby Book?" Women and new religious movements in Africa. Paper presented at the 16th congress of the international association for the history of religions, Rome, September 1990. pp 1-57.

HARRIES-JONES, P. (1975), *Freedom and labour: Mobilization and political control on the Zambian Copperbelt*. Oxford: Basil Blackwell.

HEALEY, J.G. (1981), *A fifth gospel: The experience of black Christian values*. New York: Orbis Books.

HELLMAN, E. (1964), Detribalisation and westernisation. In: Eisenstadt, S.N. (ed.), *Comparative social problems*. New York: The Free Press. pp 346-350.

HINFELAAR, H. (1989), *Religious change among the Bemba speaking women of Zambia*. London: University of London.

JONKER, C. (1992), Sleeping with the devil. *Etnofoor,* jrg. *5 (1/2)*: pp 213-233.

JULES-ROSETTE, B. (1980), Changing aspects of women's initiation in Southern Africa: An exploratory study. *Canadian journal of African studies,* Vol. *13* no *3*. Ottawa: Canadian association of African studies. pp 389-405.

— (1981), *Symbols of change: Urban transition in a Zambian community*. New Jersey: Ablex Publishing Corporation, Norwood.

LABREQUE, E. (1982), *Believes and rituals of the Bemba and neighbouring tribes*. Ilondola/Chinsali (Zambia): Language Centre. [first printed 1931-1934]

LA FONTAINE, J. (1972), Ritualization of women's life-crisis in Bugisu In: La Fontaine, J. (ed.), *The interpretation of ritual*. London: Tavistock Publications Ltd. pp 159-186.

— (1986), *Initiation*. Manchester: Manchester University Press.

LAGERWERF, L. (1984), *"They pray for you..." Independent churches and women in Botswana*. Leiden/Utrecht: Interuniversity institute for missiological and ecumenical research.

— (1990), African women doing theology - a survey. *Exchange, Journal of missiological and ecumenical research,* vol. *19* 1990 no. *1*. Leiden/Utrecht: Interuniversity institute for missiological and ecumenical research.

LINDEN, I. (1975), Chewa initiation rites and *Nyau* societies: the use of religious institutions in local politics at Mua. In: Ranger, T.O. and J. Weller (eds.), *Themes in the Christian history of central Africa*. London: Heinemann. pp 30-44.

MAUSS, M. (1972), *A general theory of magic*. London: Routledge and Kegan Paul Ltd. [first printed in 1950], Press Universitair de France.

MBITI, J.S. (1990), *African religions and philosophy*. Second edition, [first printed in 1969]. Nairobi: Heinemann Educational Books Ltd.

MITCHELL, J.C. (1969), *Social networks in urban situations*. Manchester: University Press.

MOORE, S.F. (1977), Epilogue: Uncertainties in situations, indeterminacies in culture. In: Moore, S.F. and B.G. Meyerhoff (eds.), *Symbol and politics in communal ideology: Cases and questions*. Ithaca and London: University Press. pp 210-239.

MORROW, S. (1989), "On the side of the robbed": R.J.B. Moore, missionary on the Copperbelt, 1933-1941. *Journal of religion in Africa,* Vol. *XIX 3*, Oct. 1989. Zomba (Malawi): University of Malawi. pp 244-261.

MUNACHONGA, M.L. (1989), Women and development in Zambia. In: Parpart, J. (ed.), *Women and development in Africa*. University Press of America. pp 279-311.

MUZOREWA, F.D. (1975), Through prayer to action: the Rukwadzano women of Rhodesia. In: Ranger, T.O. and J. Weller (eds.), *Themes in the Christian history of central Africa*. London: Heinemann. pp 256-268.

NON-GOVERNMENTAL ORGANIZATIONS CO-ORDINATING COMMITTEE (n.d.), *Manela*, Issue no. *1*, vol.*1*. Lusaka: NGOCC Zambia.

— (1988/1989), *Manela*, Issue no. *2*, vol.*1*. Lusaka: NGOCC Zambia.

— (1989/1990), *Manela*, Issue no. *3*. Lusaka: NGOCC Zambia.

O'SHEA, M. (1986), *Missionaries and miners*. Mission Press, Ndola, Zambia.

OGER, L. M.AFR. (1991), *"Where a scattered flock gathered"*. Ilondola. Ndola-Zambia: Mission Press.

PARPART, J.L. (1983), Class and gender on the Copperbelt: Women in Northern Rhodesian copper mining areas 1926-1964. Boston University: African Studies Centre, Working Paper no *77*.

PINA CABRAL, J DE (1992), The gods of the gentiles are demons. In: Hastup, K. (ed.), *Other histories*. London/New York: Routledge. pp 45-61.

RICHARDS, A.I. (1939), *Land, labour and diet in Northern Rhodesia*. Oxford: Oxford University Press

— (1940), *Bemba marriage and present economic conditions*. Rhodes Livingstone Institute, Northern Rhodesia.

— (1945), Pottery images or *mbusa* used at the chisungu ceremony of the Bemba people of north-eastern Rhodesia, *South African journal of science,* vol. *XLI*. pp 444-458.

— (1956), *Chisungu: A girls' initiation ceremony among the Bemba of Zambia*. London: Tavistock Publications Ltd.

ROBERTS, A.D. (1968), The political history of twentieth-century Zambia. In: Ranger, T.O. (ed.), *Aspects of central African history*. London: Heinemann Educational Books. pp 154-189.
— (1973), *A history of the Bemba: Political growth and change in north-eastern Zambia before 1900*. London: Longman Group Limited.
— (1976), *A history of Zambia*. London: Heinemann Educational Books.
ROGERS, B. (1980), *The domestication of women, discrimination in developing societies*. Bristol: J.W. Arrowsmith Ltd.
SCHNEIDER, JANE (1990), Spirits and the spirit of capitalism. In: Ellen Badone (ed.), *Religious orthodoxy and popular faith in European society*. Princeton, N.J.: Princeton Univ. Pr. pp 24-53.
SHORTER, A. (1991), *The church in the African city*. New York: Orbis Books.
SOFER, C. (1964), Community problems in urban east Africa. In: Eisenstadt, S.N. (ed.), *Comparative social problems*. New York: The Free Press. pp 342-345.
SUNDKLER, BENGT G.M. (1961), *Bantu prophets in South Africa*. Oxford: Oxford University Press.
TANGUY (1962), *The Bemba of Zambia*. Ilondola. Ndola (Zambia): Mission Press.
TEN HAVE, P. (1977), *Sociologisch veldonderzoek*. Amsterdam: Boom Meppel.
TER HAAR, G. (1991), *Spirit of Africa: The healing ministry of archbishop Milingo of Zambia*. London: Hearst and Company.
TOUWEN, A. (1990), *Socio-economic development of women in Zambia: an analysis of two women's organizations*. Leiden: African Studies Centre.
— (1984), *"I'm suffering"; a pilot study of the position of female heads-of-household in a rural Copperbelt community in Zambia*. Groningen: University of Groningen.
TURNER, V.W. (1957), *Schism and continuity in an African society: A study of Ndembu village life*. Manchester: Manchester University Press.
— (1967), *The forest of symbols*. New York: Cornell University Press.
— (1969), *The ritual process*. New York: Cornell University Press.
— (1981), Encounter with Freud: The making of a comparative symbologist. In: Spindler, G.D. (ed.), *The making of a psychological anthropologist*. University of California Press. pp 558-583.
VAN BINSBERGEN, W.M.J. (1981), *Religious change in Zambia*, London: Kegan Paul International Ltd.
— (1985), From tribe to ethnicity in western Zambia: The unit of study as an ideological problem. In: Van Binsbergen, W.M.J. and M. Doornbos (eds.), *Afrika in spiegelbeeld*. Haarlem: In de Knipscheer. pp 181-234.
— (1987a), Exploring continuity and transformation in urban Zambia: A perspective on church, party and social control in a Lusaka Township. WUOO Conference on African Towns, Leiden, 26-28 February 1985, November 1987.
— (1987b), African towns: The sociological perspective. WUOO Conference on African Towns, Leiden, 26-28 February 1985, November 1987.
— (1987c), De schaduw waar je niet overheen mag stappen: Een westers onderzoeker op het Nkoja Meisjesfeest. In: Van Binsbergen, W.M.J. and M. Doornbos (eds.), *Afrika in spiegelbeeld*. Haarlem: In de Knipscheer. pp 139-182.
— (1987d), Eerste veldwerk: Tunesië 1968. In: Van Binsbergen, W.M.J. and M. Doornbos (eds.), *Afrika in spiegelbeeld*. Haarlem: In de Knipscheer. pp 21-55.
— (1994), *WOTRO programme: Globalization and the construction of communal identities*. (unpublished)
VAN DER LANS, N. AND M. NOOTER (EDS.) (1988), *Soul sister says: Hoe vrouwen in Zambia leven*. Amsterdam: Kon. Inst. voor de Tropen.
VAN GENNEP, A. (1909), *Les rites de passage*. Paris: Librairie Critique Emile Nourry.
VAN WESEMAEL-SMIT, J.L. (1988), Autonomy and women's groups, the new key to theory and policy on women and development? In: Quarles van Ufford, P. and M. Schoffeleers, *Religion and development, towards an integrated approach*. pp 265-288.
VERSTRAELEN, F.J. (1975), *An African church in transition, from missionary dependence to mutuality in mission: A case study on the Roman-Catholic church in Zambia*. Tilburg & Leiden: Development Research Inst. Tilburg & IIMO Leiden.
— (1976), Afrikaanse christenen en "wederkerige assistentie". *Wereld en zending, Tijdschrift voor missiologie*, jrg. 5, nr. 2. pp 186-203.

VERSTRAELEN-GILHUIS, G. (1982), *From Dutch mission church to reformed church in Zambia*. The scope for African leadership and initiative in the history of a Zambian mission church. Franeker (Netherlands): T. Wever.

VUYK, T. (1990), Bloed en voedsel: jongens- en meisjesinitiatie rituelen bij de Ndembu. *Antropologische verkenningen 9* nr. *3*. pp 49-64.

WALKER, C. (1990), Gender and the development of the migrant labour system, c. 1850-1930. In: *Women and Gender in Southern Africa to 1945*. London: James Curry Ltd. pp 168-197.

WEST, M. (1975), *Bishops and prophets in a black city*. London: Rex Collings Ltd.

WHITE, C.M.N., J. CHINJAVATA AND L.E. MUKWATO (1958), Comparative aspects of Luvale female puberty ritual In: Cole D.T., J. Lewin and M.G. Marwick (eds.), *African studies*. vol. *17*. Johannesburg: Witwatersrand University Press. pp 204-220.